DANIEL

COURAGE IN CHAOS

Daniel: Courage in Chaos

ISBN 978-1-955295-12-3

COURIER PUBLISHING

Greenville, South Carolina

PUBLISHED IN THE UNITED STATES OF AMERICA

DEDICATION

I dedicate this book to my family — to my wife, Joy; our daughter, Jill, her husband, Scott, and their children: Grace, Joshua, Caleb, Elijah, Hannah, Josiah, and Luke; our son, Kenny, his wife, Sarah, and their children: Emily and Kenneth. My prayer is that as a family we will always walk with the Lord.

TABLE OF CONTENTS

FOREWORD

When you find a friend who is wise, knowledgeable, giving, and fun to be with, then you have been God blessed. Such was the case when God led me, my wife Shirley, and my children Todd and Dawn to Tulip Grove Baptist Church in Hermitage, Tennessee. Pastor Ken Clayton had the qualities I sought in a pastor. He had the credentials of a pastor, and more. He had the kind of honest warmth that made you gravitate to him. His effectiveness as a pastor and preacher/teacher gave testimony of his spiritual insights by the many church members and others who loved him and were guided by him.

Dr. Clayton's biblical knowledge is evidenced through his teaching, preaching, and writing. His deep and abiding love for our Lord is manifested by giving clarity to facts and truths in God's Word.

In *Daniel: Courage in Chaos,* you will find a great deal of historical facts with Dr. Clayton's teaching as to the meaning they have regarding conditions in the world today. Emphasized also will be the place of our Lord in the historical events.

The book is structured in outline-type form, which enables the reader to better grasp the meaning of the scriptural emphases. With Daniel being a prophetic book, the subject titles in the outline will enhance a reader's understanding of content. The chapter titles are intriguing, which will stimulate the reader to search out the content.

Mic Morrow
Retired Editor, Writer, and Consultant
Lifeway Christian Resources
Nashville, Tennessee

PREFACE

This book on Daniel is based on a series of sermons preached at Pine Eden Baptist Church in Crossville, Tennessee. An invaluable aid in preparation for the sermons and this book was Nelson's NKJV Study Bible, published by Thomas Nelson Publishers, 1982, General Editor Earl D. Radmacher, Th.D. This study Bible was essential in relating all the historical persons associated with Daniel's visions. To get the most out of this study, it would be best to have your Bible open to the proper passage in Daniel. Read the passage from the Bible as you read the material from this book.

Introduction

BACKGROUND

The reign of King Nabopolassar of Babylon was marked by his defeat of the Assyrian Empire. Nabopolassar died in 605 BC after making the Babylonian Empire the dominant world force. The Northern Kingdom of Israel had already fallen to the Assyrians in 722 BC. In 605 BC, King Jehoiakim of Judah came under the control of Babylon. When Nebuchadnezzar succeeded his father Nabopolassar, he started the process of removing the "cream of the crop" people from Judah and taking them to Babylon.

What caused the Lord's judgment to come upon the nations of Israel and Judah? It began with Solomon. Solomon began as a good king, but in his last days he "turned from the Lord" (1 Kings 11). Solomon, supposedly a wise man, married 700 wives and allowed them to worship their idols. This led to rapidly declining moral behavior and a turning away from the Lord. After Solomon's death, the kingdom was divided. The wicked Northern Kingdom was conquered by the Assyrians in 722 BC. The Southern Kingdom of Judah, which had some God-fearing, God-serving kings, soon followed this downward moral spiral and was conquered by Babylon in 605 BC.

DANIEL'S CHAOTIC LIFE

Can you imagine the chaos a young person like Daniel must have experienced? What happened to his family? Daniel was uprooted from his old familiar surroundings and traveled across the desert to the large city of Babylon. The language was different, the customs were different, the religion was different, and the food was different. All that Daniel had known was gone. Daniel was separated from the Temple, separated from Jerusalem, his family, his friends, and his old neighborhood.

How did Daniel not only survive, but thrive in the midst of this chaos? In the chaos Daniel exhibited great courage. Where did that courage come from?

Daniel's courage came from his faith in Almighty God. In the first part of the Book of Daniel, we see the faith of Daniel exhibited in extreme circumstances. Daniel was taken captive to Babylon in 605 BC. Daniel referred to Cyrus (Daniel 6:28), so a date for the writing of the Book of Daniel was around 530 BC. Daniel was inspired to write about future events in the latter part of the book. Daniel wanted others to know that the Lord God Almighty was the only true God and that He ruled in the affairs of humanity. Daniel looked forward to the time when the Lord would gather His people and establish the kingdom of the Messiah. History truly is "His story." The Lord is in charge!

I was moved to write about Daniel when I realized the amazing similarities between Daniel's time and now. The amazing connection is the chaos that has enveloped America.

CHAOS IN AMERICA

1) Riots. The summer of 2020 was filled with riots in major American cities from coast to coast. Over two thousand police officers were injured in those riots. Riots continued in Portland, Oregon for months. Because of the "defund the police" movement, no bail required, the early release of prisoners or no jail sentence at all, the crime rate in America is soaring. More than four hundred police officers have left the police force in Chicago. In some cities, the prosecutors are prosecuting the police instead of the criminals. Many declare that the criminals are the victims, not the people they harm.

2) Violence. There have been over ten thousand shootings in the first six months of 2021. Shootings are up in New York City sixty-seven percent. Shootings are up one hundred forty-two percent in Chicago. Seventy percent of businesses in major cities are hiring private security guards to protect their stores. Road rage shootings have doubled over the past four years.

Inflation is surging. For example, the cost of gasoline is up forty percent and the cost of all products are rising.

3)   *Critical race theory.* This is being taught to our military, in corporations, and throughout many educational systems from college level down to kindergarten. Critical race theory is being taught in fifty school districts in fifteen states to four- and five-year-olds. Basically, it teaches race hate and that being white is evil. White is a place of privilege and is the oppressor. People of color are seen as the oppressed. People of color are victims and have no chance of change according to critical race theory. This is Marxist teaching that is trying to divide Americans along racial lines. Dr. Martin Luther King, in his famous "I Have a Dream" speech, longed for the day in America when a person would be judged based on his character and not the color of their skin. Today, many politicians are pushing the idea that we should judge and categorize everyone according to color.

America is in chaos! What should we do as believers? What did Daniel do? Tucker Carlson has a special on Fox News entitled "Surviving Disorder." How did Daniel survive disorder, and how can we survive disorder today?

DANIEL

COURAGE IN CHAOS

KEN CLAYTON

CHAPTER 1

DANIEL OBEYS GOD
DANIEL 1:1-18

THE BACKGROUND

Daniel in verse 1 began his account of the Babylonian captivity of the Jewish people by giving the date as the third year of the reign of King Jehoiachin of Judah (2 Kings 24:10-17). The king of Babylon, Nebuchadnezzar, besieged Jerusalem. Daniel emphasized the rule of God over the nations. Jerusalem fell because of their disobedience and idolatry, so God judged them (v. 2). Some of the articles from the Temple were taken to Shinar (Babylon) and placed in a pagan temple. This portrayed the total dominance of Babylon over Judah. God had ordained Babylon "for judgment" and "marked them for correction" (Habakkuk 1:12).

God is in charge! Today, we need to know that, understand that, and believe that God is in charge!

CONTROLLING THE MINDS OF YOUTH

Nebuchadnezzar was a powerful dictator. He had the power to put anyone to death and spare others (Daniel 1:3-4). Young men of noble birth, intelligence, and who were good-looking were picked to be trained to serve the king.

Today, political leaders understand the power gained by controlling the education and training of our children and youth. Many today are seeking to teach critical race theory, blotting out America's history, and charting a more socialistic future for America. It is so important for parents to monitor television and communication media, video games, movies, and books their children read so they can give their children guidance. Our pagan society bombards our culture constantly, seeking to lure youth away from faith in Christ.

The chosen youth were to be trained for three years in the language, culture, and the religion of Babylon (Daniel 1:5).

How would the Babylonians control
the minds of the youth?

1) The Jews would be awestruck at the power of Babylon. The city wall was a perfect square, fifteen miles on each side. The wall was eighty-seven feet thick and three hundred and eighty-seven feet high. They channeled the Euphrates River through the city. It was a city of two million people. The Hanging Gardens of Babylon was one of the Seven Wonders of the ancient world. It was a highly developed intellectual center.

2) The Jewish youth would be tempted with the good life. They were to have all the best to eat and drink and live in the palace (Daniel 1:5). One of the greatest temptations young people face today is to seek the life of the "rich and famous." "The good life" and "party hardy" is the call of our society today to young people.

3) The Jewish youth received a new name (Daniel 1:6-7). In order to change their history and their identity they were given new names. Daniel, which means "God is my judge," was changed to "Belteshazzar," meaning "Bel protect his life." Daniel's three close friends' name changes were: Hananiah, meaning "Yahweh is gracious," was changed to

Shadrach, meaning "under the command of Aku" (moon god); Mishael, meaning "Who is what God is?" was changed to Meshach, meaning "I am of little account"; and Azariah, meaning "Yahweh has helped me," was changed to Abed-nego, meaning "Servant of Nebo" (a god).

Today, when young people graduate or move away from home, they often forget who they are, where they came from, and to whom they belong. As a result, many young people stop attending church. Satan and this pagan world are trying to pull our youth away, so they will forget their Christian teachings.

The name changes were an attempt by the Babylonians to erase their Jewish history, teaching, and worship of the Lord.

DANIEL'S RESPONSE

In verse 4, Daniel and the other Jewish captives that were to be trained were called "youth." The word was used to designate teenagers from fourteen to seventeen years old. Can you imagine a young teenager standing up to all these temptations and saying "NO!" (Daniel 1:8)? Daniel was determined to serve the Lord, and he refused to serve the gods of Babylon. The food was unclean, having been offered to idols.

It is so easy for youth to go along with the crowd. They can make excuses like "Everybody is doing it," or "My parents will never know," or "I want to be popular." No matter what the excuse, sin is sin. Bowing down before anyone or anything except the Lord God is sin! Compromising God's Word is sin.

Daniel also offered a solution (Daniel 1:12-14). Daniel talked to Ashpenaz, the chief of the king's eunuchs (Daniel 1:9-10). Ashpenaz was afraid to go against the king's command. So Daniel spoke with the steward whom Ashpenaz had placed over Daniel and his three friends (Daniel 1:11). Daniel proposed a ten-day test. They would drink only water and eat "vegetables" (Daniel 1:12-14). The word "vegetables" can mean anything grown in the ground. This could have referred to grains also.

In Ezekiel 4:9 are instructions for making bread using "wheat, barley, beans lentils, millet, and spelt." You can buy today a cereal named "Ezekiel 4:9" that includes these ingredients.

THE RESULT

At the end of ten days, they were healthier than the young men who ate the king's delicacies (Daniel 1:15). So that became their diet for the rest of their training (Daniel 1:16-17). When the three-year training period was over, and the king examined them, Daniel and his three friends were the top of the class (Daniel 1:18-20).

They did better than all the others because the Lord "gave them knowledge and skill in all literature and wisdom; and Daniel had understanding in all visions and dreams" (Daniel 1:17).

WILL YOU BE LIKE DANIEL?

Daniel would not compromise his faith in the Lord. Even if it seemed like a small thing to eat and drink the delicacies of the king rather than honor God in what he ate and drank. Daniel survived chaos because he obeyed the Lord.

Our challenge today is to stand true to the Lord Jesus Christ. The world wants you to bend God's rules in order to get ahead or to live the "good life." Except for our Lord Jesus Christ, Daniel is the only person in scripture that continually gave a faithful testimony to the Lord all his life!

Will you be like Daniel today?

Nebuchadnezzar's Dream
Daniel 2:1-49

Daniel was a prophet in the Babylonian Empire, one of the most powerful of ancient times. Yet, it too fell, like hundreds of nations of the past. The rise and fall of nations may seem like the natural ebb and flow of history. But Daniel declared that God "removes kings and raises up kings" (Daniel 2:21). Earthly kingdoms are temporary, while the coming kingdom of God "shall never be destroyed" (Daniel 2:44).

King Nebuchadnezzar reigned in Babylon from 605 to 562 BC. He is the most significant Gentile king mentioned in the Bible. His name appears in scripture about ninety times.

Chapter 2 of Daniel recorded God speaking in a dream to the king. God was revealing His plan for the Gentile nations. This is one of the most revealing prophetic pictures predicting the future of four empires: Babylon, Medes and Persians, Greece, and Rome. It outlines the return of the Roman empire at the end of time and the coming of Christ's eternal kingdom.

The King's Dream

After King Nebuchadnezzar had conquered all his enemies, he had trouble sleeping (Daniel 2:1). He was "troubled" or "deeply disturbed."

Then the king commanded that all the "magicians, astrologers, sorcerers, and Chaldeans (wise men)" come and tell him his dream (Daniel 2:2).

Then the Chaldeans announced in Aramaic that the king should tell them his dream, and then they would give an interpretation (Daniel 2:4). Aramaic was the most common language of the day. Daniel 2:4b-7:8 is written in Aramaic.

1) *The command.* The king wanted to be certain of the interpretation so he apparently was suspicious of their ability. So, he commanded that they tell him the dream and its interpretation, or they would be "cut in pieces" and their home burned (Daniel 2:5). If they were able to do as the king commanded, they would be richly rewarded (Daniel 2:6).

2) *The King's counselors responded.* Again, they asked the king to tell them his dream (Daniel 2:7). The king realized they were stalling for time and again commanded them to tell him his dream first because he felt they had agreed together to lie to him (Daniel 2:7-9).

The Chaldeans replied that none of them, nor any king, lord, or ruler ever asked such a thing, and there is "no other who can tell it to the king except the gods" (Daniel 2:10-11).

3) *The king's decree.* The king was furious and commanded that all of the wise men of Babylon be destroyed. When the decree went out, Daniel and his friends were also in danger (Daniel 2:12-13). So Daniel spoke to Arioch, the captain of the king's guard, to discover what was happening (Daniel 2:14-15). Then Daniel went straight to the king to ask for some time. Then he would tell the king the interpretation (Daniel 2:16).

4) *Prayer.* Daniel went home and told Hananiah, Mishael, and Azariah that they must seek mercy from the "God of heaven" to learn the secret of the dream (Daniel 2:17-18). Daniel, despite his education and wisdom, knew what you and I ought to know; that prayer to Almighty God is the first step in a chaotic situation. Daniel did not pray alone, but

gathered his close friends to pray with him.

The title "God of heaven" is used frequently in the later books of the Old Testament. The title expresses the rule of God over the nations.

5) *Praise.* God revealed the secret to Daniel in a "night vision," and Daniel praised the Lord. Normally visions occurred in the daytime and dreams at night. Daniel praised God because He is in control. He changes the times and the seasons. God controls the nations as "He removes kings and raises up kings." God is the source of wisdom, knowledge, and understanding. Daniel also praised God for revealing the dream and interpretation to him (Daniel 2:19-23).

DANIEL AND THE KING

Daniel first went to Arioch to stop the destruction of the wise men of Babylon by telling him that he knew the interpretation. Arioch brought Daniel to the king. Daniel explained that humans could not tell the king his dream, "but there is a God in heaven who reveals secrets" (Daniel 2:24-28). We can trust in the Lord to help us in our time of need.

A) *Daniel gave all the credit to the Lord and took none for himself.* We should always give all the glory to God and not brag on our efforts (Daniel 2:28).

B) *God is in control.* There may be times when you are worried or concerned. You may take your troubles to bed with you, like Nebuchadnezzar. But we must trust in the love, wisdom, and power of the Lord (Daniel 2:29).

C) *Since the whole world is in God's hands* (Job 38:3-11) means that you are in His hands as well. When you feel overwhelmed, place your problems in the Lord's hands.

D) *Like Daniel, we need to pray.* There is the power of the Holy Spirit involved in our prayers (Romans 8:26). Daniel enlisted his friends to join him in prayer. We need to have times of prayer with fellow believers.

DANIEL REVEALED THE DREAM

In order to understand what the Bible teaches about the future, this chapter (Daniel 2:37-45) is a good place to start. King Nebuchadnezzar dreamed of a high statue that decreased in value from its head down to its feet (Daniel 2:31-33). No human kingdom is permanent. All human kingdoms will fall when Jesus brings in His eternal kingdom. This dream was a message of hope to God's people about the final outcome of history. Daniel described the dream in verses 31-36.

DANIEL INTERPRETED THE DREAM

1) Babylon is the head of gold (Daniel 2:37-38). Daniel started at the top of the statue with Babylon. Babylon's rule lasted until 539 BC. Why was Babylon represented by gold? One hundred years after Nebuchadnezzar, a Greek historian wrote about the large supply of gold in Babylon. The prophet Jeremiah wrote: "Babylon was a golden cup in the Lord's hand ... Babylon has suddenly fallen and been destroyed" (Jeremiah 51:7-8).

Babylon was, of course, the current existing world power, so Nebuchadnezzar's God-given dream began there.

2) The Medes and the Persians are the chest and arms (Daniel 2:39). The next kingdom is not as powerful and is represented by silver. The two arms represented the two divisions of the kingdom — the Medes and the Persians. They ruled for 200 years until 331 BC.

3) Greece is the belly and thighs of bronze (Daniel 2:39). The next kingdom was started by Phillip of Macedonia and later his famous son, Alexander the Great. Why would bronze refer to Greece? Possibly it was because Alexander the Great equipped his army with helmets, breastplates, shields and swords made out of bronze.

4) Rome is the legs of iron (Daniel 2:40). Rome conquered Greece. Their weapons were made of iron. Iron is used fourteen times in Daniel.

The Romans crushed all who came before them. Daniel's vision in Chapter 7, verse 7 refers to Rome as a beast with "iron teeth." Remember, it was Rome that ruled the world in the time of the New Testament.

5) *The ten-kingdom group represented by feet and toes of clay and iron* (Daniel 2:41-43). The two "iron legs" (Daniel 2:33) could refer to the split that occurred in the Roman Empire. The eastern empire had as its capital Istanbul, and the western empire's capital was Rome.

To what in history could the feet and toes refer? Nothing in the past fits this description. This part of the prophecy is still in the future. Many think this is some form of the Roman Empire that will exist when God sets up His earthly kingdom (Daniel 2:44). Some have compared this to the European Common Market or perhaps NATO.

Where does the United States fit into this prophecy? First, you must assume that the United States will still exist when Christ comes again. If the United States does exist, it has trade agreements with the Common Market, and alliances with the NATO nations. Also, the early colonists were mainly from European nations. So the United States could relate in these ways.

6) *The final kingdom of Christ.* "(A) stone was cut out without hands, which struck the image on its feet of iron and clay, and broke then in pieces." (Daniel 2:34). The stone destroyed the kingdoms of men and then became a great mountain that filled the earth (Daniel 2:35).

The explanation of the stone is given in verse 45: "And in the days of these kings the God of heaven will set up a kingdom which shall never be destroyed ..." (Daniel 2:44). "(T)he great god has made known to the king what will come to pass after this. The dream is certain, and its interpretation is sure" (Daniel 2:45).

Jesus is called "the stone" by Peter when he addressed the Sanhedrin: "This is the stone which was rejected by you builders, which has become the chief cornerstone" (Acts 4:11).

RESULTS OF DANIEL'S DREAM INTERPRETATION

1) Nebuchadnezzar thanked Daniel (Daniel 2:46).

2) Nebuchadnezzar praised God. "Truly your God is the God of gods, the Lord of kings and a revealer of secrets ..." (Daniel 2:47).

3) Nebuchadnezzar promoted Daniel. "(A)nd he made him ruler over the whole province of Babylon, and chief administrator over all the wise men of Babylon" (Daniel 2:48).

4) Nebuchadnezzar promoted Daniel's three friends. Shadrach, Meshach, and Abed-Nego were placed over the affairs of the province of Babylon (Daniel 2:49).

5) The dream revealed the decreasing stability, the declining morality and the decreasing unity of human government. The toes and feet are partly clay and partly iron, which means these governments will be partly strong and partly fragile (Daniel 2:41-43).

WHAT DOES NEBUCHADNEZZAR'S DREAM REVEAL TO US ABOUT CHRIST'S COMING KINGDOM?

1) Christ's kingdom is supernatural. It is represented as a "stone cut without hands" that will be "set up by the God of heaven" (Daniel 2:34, 44).

2) Christ's kingdom will come suddenly. The supernatural stone *"struck the feet and broke them into pieces"* (Daniel 2:34). This was a sudden striking, not a gradual decline in the power of the nations. Peter said that Jesus was coming as a "thief in the night" (2 Peter 3:10). Paul wrote that Jesus would come "in a moment, in the twinkling of an eye" (1 Corinthians 15:52).

3) Christ's kingdom will be victorious. This is how we know that Daniel's prophecy is revealing the coming of Christ's kingdom, because it will be a "kingdom which shall never be destroyed" (Daniel 2:44).

4) Christ's kingdom will bring judgment. The kingdoms of this world will be "crushed together and become like chaff from the summer threshing floor; the wind carried them away so that no trace of them was found." (Daniel 2:35)

5) Christ's kingdom will rule the world. The "stone ... became a great mountain and filled the whole earth" (Daniel 2:35). In Jesus' model prayer that He gave the disciples, they were taught to pray: "Your kingdom come, your will be done on earth as it is in heaven" (Matthew 6:10).

WHAT DOES DANIEL CHAPTER 2 MEAN FOR YOU TODAY?

1) When you face chaotic times, don't lose courage. Don't lose faith. Daniel kept his faith in the Lord and the Lord gave Daniel the courage to face every situation.

2) When you learn of the rising crime rate, chaos in the streets, the bad actions of rogue nations, remember there is our God in heaven. The Lord is in control of history, He is in control of our future, and one day Jesus will return and set up His eternal kingdom.

Whatever happens in this world, Christ assures us of a blessed future, because He is in charge. "Let not your heart be troubled; you believe in God, believe also in Me" (John 14:1).

CHAPTER 3

But If Not

Daniel 3

The Cuban people recently (2021) have been in the streets peacefully protesting the oppression and tyranny of the communist government. Most Americans have not experienced living in a country where you have no rights, where you are ruled over by all powerful dictators. The people of Judah had been taken into captivity in Babylon and were under the absolute control of the ruler Nebuchadnezzar. The king attempted to kill three of his valuable advisors because they defied his command to worship his golden image.

This type of ruthlessness still occurs in our day. When Isis began to take over in Iraq in 2014, they gave Christians an order. They must convert to Islam, leave the country, or die. Many Christians have literally lost their heads because they stayed true to Christ.

Will you remain strong in the face of overwhelming pressure from the media, Hollywood, and some politicians to convert Christians to a non-moral worldview? Will you stand true to Christ or deny Him?

Chapter 3 of Daniel is a powerful account of courage and faith in response to the orders of a tyrannical leader to bow down and worship an idol instead of the One and True Lord God Almighty.

THE IMAGE OF GOLD

King Nebuchadnezzar demanded the whole nation to worship an idol. Why would he do this? The king may have thought he could better unify his kingdom around a central worship place and a central worship figure.

So the king ordered a massive gold image to be set up in the Plain of Dura about six miles southeast of the city of Babylon. The word "image" means it was in human form. The size of the image was "sixty cubits by six cubits" (Daniel 3:1). In Israel a cubit was the distance from the elbow to the tip of the fingers, or about eighteen inches. In Babylon a cubit was about twenty inches. King Nebuchadnezzar's image was ninety to one hundred feet tall and about nine or ten feet wide. In contrast, the Statue of Liberty in New York harbor is 151 feet tall (not including the pedestal and foundation).

THE COMMAND

When the time came for the dedication of the image, Nebuchadnezzar "sent word" to gather all the governmental leaders and officials to come to the dedication (Daniel 3:2). This was a demand. ALL who were invited were required to attend, no excuses. When they all had gathered, it was proclaimed that when they heard the musicians play, they were all to "fall down and worship the image" (Daniel 3:3-5).

The second part of the command was that if anyone did not obey and fall down and worship the image, they would be immediately put into a "burning fiery furnace" (Daniel 3:6).

THE REFUSAL

When the multitude heard the music, they all fell down and worshiped the golden image. (Daniel 3:7) Everyone worshiped the image, except for three captive Hebrews. Some of Nebuchadnezzar's advisors who were jealous of Daniel and his tree friends had watched carefully to see how they would react. Apparently, Daniel was not there, but Shadrach, Meshach, and Abed-Nego did not worship the image. So they reported to the king and reminded the king of his command and informed him that three of the Jews did not worship the image (Daniel 3:8-12).

Then the king, in "rage and fury," commanded that the three be brought before him (Daniel 3:13). The king asked, "Is it true ..." that they failed to worship the image? Do you deny it? Do you confess it? The king was willing to give the Jews a second chance. When you hear the music, bow down. If not, you will die in the furnace (Daniel 3:15). Then the king threw this challenge into the face of God: "And who is the god who will deliver you from my hands" (Daniel 3:15).

THE ANSWER

Shadrach, Meshach, and Abed-Nego responded, "We have no need to answer you in this matter" (Daniel 3:16). Why did they say that? They knew the commands of God. They were not to make a carved image or have any other gods (Ex. 20:3-4). No decision necessary. The matter was already settled. They already knew what they should do. They understood that faithfulness to God required that they would never worship another god.

The answer of Daniel's three friends really has three parts:

1) *We will not bow down to the image.*

2) *They also answered that:* "Our God whom we serve is able to deliver us ..." (Daniel 3:17). They believed that God was all powerful. The angel asked Sarah; "Is anything too hard for the Lord?" (Genesis 18:14). Jesus said to the disciples: "With men this is impossible, but with God all things are possible" (Matthew 19:26). Jude wrote: "Now

to Him who is able to keep you from stumbling, and to present you faultless before the presence of His glory with exceeding joy ..." (Jude 24). Shadrach, Meshach, and Abed-Nego knew their God was able to deliver them!

3) "But if not ..." (Daniel 3:18). They were not questioning God's power, but they were placing their lives in the hands of God. Jesus, in the garden of Gethsemane, prayed, "Not my will, but thine be done" (Luke 22:42). Their faith was being put to an extreme test, yet they remained committed to the will of God, no matter what happened! They did not ask for a miracle, but trusted in the Lord who was in control.

God is able to deliver, but in this particular case it may not be His will to deliver us. And even if it is not His will to deliver us, "let it be known to you Oh, king, that we do not serve your gods, nor will we worship the gold image which you have set up" (Daniel 3:18).

The Fiery Furnace

1) The king became so angry that he ordered the furnace to be heated seven times hotter than normal (Daniel 3:19). When you are filled with fury, you are filled with folly. The king lost his temper, and he lost all sense of kindness and rational thought. He ordered the three Jews to be burned alive (Daniel 3:20). When the king had the three Jews thrown into the furnace, it was so hot that the men who were putting them in the furnace all died from the heat (Daniel 3:21-22). The "mighty men of valor" were the king's personal bodyguards.

2) The king was astonished when he realized there were four men in the fire, and "the fourth is like the Son of God" (Daniel 3:24-25). All four were loose and walking around in the fire!

3) The king called for the three, Shadrach, Meshach, and Abed-Nego to come out of the furnace. The king remembered that the Hebrews were servants of the "Most High God" (Daniel 3:26).

4) All the government officials gathered around, and "they saw these men on whose bodies the fire had no power." Their garments were not affected; there was no smell of smoke on them, and their hair was not even singed (Daniel 3:27).

5) The king praised God. The king praised God because He "delivered His servants who trusted in Him"; because thereby God had frustrated the king's order; and proved that they should "not serve or worship any god except their own God! (Daniel 3:28). The king added: "… there is no other God who can deliver like this" (Daniel 3:29). Pagans did not deny the existence of many gods. Nebuchadnezzar was not proclaiming faith in God, but he did at least acknowledge that the God of the Jews was able to deliver His followers, and the king made a decree that no one should speak against their God (Daniel 3:29).

LESSONS FROM DANIEL CHAPTER 3 FOR TODAY

1) Shadrach, Meshach, and Abed-Nego stood up for their faith, even when the penalty was death. What a great example for us of courage in chaos, courage under fire!

2) Our God is able. No matter what the situation we can declare: "Our God is able!" "Now to Him who is able to establish you according to my gospel and the preaching of Jesus Christ, according to the revelation of the mystery kept secret since the world began … to God, alone wise, be glory through Jesus Christ forever" (Romans 16:25, 27).

3) "But if not …" (Daniel 3:18). We must learn to stay true to the will of God for our lives whether we are delivered from every trial or not. If it is not God's will to deliver me on my time schedule or in my way, I must still trust His will and purpose for my life.

4) Decision made. We must determine in advance of any situation that we are going to remain faithful to our Lord Jesus Christ.

I have counseled young people and adults over the years not to wait until you are offered liquor, drugs, or sex to decide whether or not you will give in to the temptation. Take your stand ahead of time. Don't be a cowardly Christian. Faithful Christians must have the courage in the midst of chaos to take their stand with Jesus.

The three Hebrew youth said: "We have no need to answer you in this matter" (Daniel 3:16). Why not? They had decided already! Their minds were already made up!

These three heroes in Daniel Chapter 3 experienced a promise the Lord made to Isaiah many years earlier: "Fear not, for I have redeemed you; I have called you by your name; you are Mine. When you pass through the waters, I will be with you; and through the rivers, they shall not overflow you. When you walk through the fire, you shall not be burned, nor shall the flame scorch you. For I am the Lord your God, the Holy One of Israel, your Savior" (Isaiah 43:1-3).

CHAPTER 4

O, How The Mighty Have Fallen!
Daniel 4:1-37

Simone Biles, arguably the greatest female gymnast of all time, dropped out of several events during the 2020 Tokyo Olympics because of mental issues. She returned to competition and won the bronze medal on the balance beam. She explained that she dropped out of several events because her body and mind were not in sync.

The chaotic world in which we live, with all the stressors that go with it, can lead to mental health problems. Stress can be a leading factor in blood pressure, heart problems, and kidney problems.

Stress and other mental issues can also be a factor in suicide. There are one thousand suicides in Tennessee every year on average. Across the nation, the pandemic, economic problems, and the lockdowns have led to increases in suicide, even among children.

In the fourth chapter of Daniel is the unusual story of King Nebuchadnezzar. The king was very wealthy. The kingdom was the most powerful in the world. And the king thought he didn't need God or anybody else. The king was overcome with a mental illness designed by the Lord to humble him.

Unlike other chapters in Daniel, this one appears to be the king's testimony, much of the chapter is written from his point of view. For example, in verse 4 the king wrote, "I, Nebuchadnezzar, was at my rest … ."

NEBUCHADNEZZAR'S SECOND DREAM

1) The king's testimony is in the form of a letter to "all peoples, nations, and languages" (Daniel 4:1). The purpose of his letter was to "declare the signs and wonders that the Most High God has worked for me." The king then praised the great and mighty signs and wonders of God and God's everlasting kingdom and dominion (Daniel 4:3). The king then began his testimony.

2) The dream described. The king was resting in his palace, and he had a fearful and troubling dream (Daniel 4:4-5). So he called together all his counselors, but they were unable to explain the dream (Daniel 4:6-7). When Daniel arrived before the king, the king expressed his confidence in Daniel: "I know that the Spirit of the Holy God is in you" (Daniel 4:9). Wouldn't it be wonderful, if we lived our lives so that people would recognize that we belong to the Lord?

Nebuchadnezzar described his dream (Daniel 4:10-17). The dream was about a great tree that "reached to the heavens" (Daniel 4:11). It had leaves and fruit in abundance, and birds lived in the tree and animals lived under the tree (Daniel 4:12). Then "a holy one" came from heaven and commanded that the tree be chopped down (Daniel 4:13-14). The stump was to be bound with a "band of bronze and iron" (Daniel 4:15). Then the stump was seen to be a symbol for a person, for he said: "And let him graze with the beasts" and "let his heart be changed" from a man to a beast (Daniel 4:16). The number seven in verse 16 is a symbol for completion. The idea was that the king would be in that condition until God had completed what He desired to do in the king's heart and mind.

That point was made clear in verse 17: "In order that the living may know that the Most High rules in the kingdom of men."

3) The dream was explained. The king then asked Daniel for an explanation (Daniel 4:18). As Daniel began his explanation, he quickly moved to reveal the main thought: The great tree represented the king: "… it is you, O King" (Daniel 4:22). Daniel wished that the dream was intended for his enemies and not the king (Daniel 4:19). In the Old Testament a tree can be a symbol for a ruler (Judges 9:7-15, Ezekiel 31:2-14, Zechariah 11:1-2). There were not many trees in Babylon, so a gigantic tree would be important.

The king was an important ruler, but he would be brought low and become as a beast of the field (Daniel 4:25). The dream was a call for repentance. "(B)reak off your sins by being righteous and your iniquities by showing mercy to the poor …" (Daniel 4:27). The purpose of these events is to convince the king that "the Most High rules in the kingdom of men, and gives it to whomever He chooses" (Daniel 4:25).

4) The dream was fulfilled. "All this came upon King Nebuchadnezzar" (Daniel 4:28). The king had twelve months to repent. He had time to change his life (Daniel 4:29). But he did not. In his pride he said, "I have built by my mighty power and for the honor of my majesty" (Daniel 4:30). In his arrogant pride he was bragging and taking credit for the greatness of Babylon.

When you start talking arrogantly about who you are and what you have done, you better be ready for the judgment of the Lord. The big "I" is the essence of sin. So many people today believe life is all about them — their needs, their wants, their desires. Their total focus is on themselves and they, like the king, become a beast! (Daniel 4:33).

5) The king praised the Lord. Seven years later (Daniel 4:25), the king made a dramatic change in his life. Instead of focusing on himself, he looked up his eyes to heaven (Daniel 4:34). When he focused on God

Most High, his sanity was restored: "… my understanding returned to me …" (Daniel 4:34). And then he began praising and honoring the Most High, "(f)or His dominion is an everlasting dominion …" (Daniel 4:34-35).

The kingdom and all the power and authority of the kingdom was restored to the king (Daniel 4:36). The king had learned his lesson, as he clearly declared: "Now I, Nebuchadnezzar, praise and extol and honor the King of heaven, all of whose works are truth, and His ways justice. And those who walk in pride He is able to put down" (Daniel 4:37).

LESSONS FOR TODAY

1) *Nebuchadnezzar learned that all of God's works are truth* (Daniel 4:37). He learned that the Lord God had an everlasting dominion (Daniel 4:34). Have you come to the point where you believe that the Lord is in control and rules over all His creation? Can you look back at your life and thank God for what you have learned even though at times it was painful? Everything the Lord does is truth, and is the best for you.

2) *Nebuchadnezzar learned that prideful people will be humbled* (Daniel 4:37). Only the Lord can cure us of "Meism." In order to take the focus off of ourselves, first focus on the Lord, which enables us to also focus on others. You begin by accepting Jesus as Lord of your life. Then stop trying to be the god of your life. Truly make Jesus Lord. Jesus must come first in your life. We must be humble before the Lord, living a prideful life is insanity.

3) *Nebuchadnezzar learned there is judgment in this world* (Daniel 4:23). We do "reap what we sow." The desire is to remove our sin from us. As a sculptor chisels away at a stone to produce a beautiful statue, the Lord cuts away our sin to make us pure in His sight.

4) *Nebuchadnezzar learned the purpose of God's judgment.* The purpose of the judgment was that the king would know who God is and

that God rules over the world. God is in charge. What will it take in your life to help you realize that you are not the center of the universe? What would have to happen for you to realize that God Almighty rules and that one day we will all face His judgment?

5) Nebuchadnezzar learned there is hope. Nebuchadnezzar was a pagan who did not know or worship the Lord. Yet, when God got through with him, he sounded like Billy Graham in an evangelistic crusade!

There is hope for those who are far away from God today. There is hope for all those who will call upon the name of the Lord (Romans 10:13).

Your salvation is at hand — not tomorrow, but today. Now you can give your life to Jesus and confess Him as your Lord and Savior. Why not now? You can admit your sin to Jesus, ask for His forgiveness, and trust Him with your life and your future.

CHAPTER 5

THE FINGERS OF GOD
DANIEL 5:1-31

As we come to the fifth chapter of Daniel, seventy years have passed since Daniel was taken in captivity to Babylon. About twenty-five years have passed since the end of Chapter 4. King Nebuchadnezzar has died after ruling for forty-four years and his grandson Belshazzar is ruling as king. Nebuchadnezzar was called Belshazzar's "father" in verse 2 that indicated that Nebuchadnezzar was an ancestor of Belshazzar. It is possible he served when Nebuchadnezzar's insanity began.

This powerful account of God's judgment upon the sin of King Belshazzar is a vivid reminder to us today that the judgment of God is only one breath away. The time will come when you will be weighed in the scales of God. What will be the result?

THE GREAT FEAST

The passage begins with a feast in a massive banquet hall. Archaeologists have found the ruins of a large room fifty-two feet wide and one hundred and seventy feet long. This room would have been large enough for "a thousand of his lords" and all the servers (Daniel 5:1).

1) *Wine, women, and song.* Drinking wine is mentioned in verses

one, two, and four. In Near Eastern culture the king did not drink wine in public. Normally, men and women had little public association. They were usually separated on social occasions, but men and women were present. Verses two and three mention "his wives and his concubines drank from them."

Apparently, they joined their voices together and praised their gods. "They drank wine, and praised the gods of gold and silver, bronze and iron, wood and stone" (Daniel 5:4). The picture is of a pagan, drunken orgy.

2) Arrogance. In those days when one country conquered another, all valuables were seized. The conquerors would loot their temple to show the superiority of their gods over those of the conquered. Belshazzar ordered that the gold and silver vessels captured in Jerusalem be brought to the banquet hall so that they might drink from them. This demonstrated an arrogance and pride that totally blasphemed the Lord God.

Their arrogance was also revealed in that they knew that Cyrus and his army were outside the walls of Babylon, but they were having a party! They were trusting in their huge walls, the Euphrates River flowing through the city, and many gardens supplying food.

THE HANDWRITING ON THE WALL

In the midst of the party-goers praising their gods, "the fingers of a man's hand appeared and wrote … on the plaster of the wall of the king's palace; and the king saw the part of the hand that wrote" (Daniel 5:5). People still use the expression: "the handwriting on the wall" when problems come, and they realize they should have seen those problems coming.

1) The king's reaction. The king must have sobered up quickly. The description of the king's reaction in verse 6 all happened at once.

First, his "countenance changed." We would probably say today that he was "white as a sheet." Second, the king's "thoughts troubled him." Having seen the fingers of a man's hand and words written on the wall, we might describe the king as "scared to death." Third, "the joints of his hips were loosened and his knees knocked against each other." The king was trembling all over! We still use the expression "their knees are knocking" about someone who is scared. The king's legs were not supporting him. All of these things together are signs of extreme fear.

2) *The king's fearful cry.* "The king cried aloud to bring in the astrologers, the Chaldeans, and the soothsayers." (Daniel 5:7). The king immediately wanted the wise men to read the writing and give an interpretation. Anyone who could do so would be richly rewarded. They would be "clothed with purple and have a chain of gold around his neck; and he shall be the third ruler in the kingdom" (Daniel 5:7).

But the wise men were not able to do what the king wanted (Daniel 5:8). The words were written in Aramaic, their language. They knew the words, but they could not understand the message. The king was then not just "troubled" but "greatly troubled," and his countenance was so changed that his "lords were astonished" (Daniel 5:9).

3) *The queen's advice.* The queen was not Belshazzar's wife, but the queen mother. She was either the daughter of Nebuchadnezzar who had married Nabonidus, the current king, Belshazzar's father. Nabonidus was king in Arabia and Belshazzar was his vice-regent. The queen may also have been Nebuchadnezzar's wife.

When the queen mother heard the commotion, she came to the banquet hall. She had not been a part of the drunken party (Daniel 5:10). The queen remembered Daniel, "in whom is the Spirit of the Holy God" (Daniel 5:11). She reminded Belshazzar that Daniel had shown much wisdom in the days of Nebuchadnezzar so that the king had made him chief of all the wise men of Babylon (Daniel 5:11). She heaped praise on

Daniel, declaring that he was "excellent … in explaining enigmas …" (Daniel 5:12). The word "explain" literally means "to untie" or "to loose." Daniel could understand and solve the dreams and visions. Daniel also always gave God the credit for his insight (Daniel 2:28). The queen told the king to call Daniel, and "he will give the interpretation" (Daniel 5:12).

4) Daniel summoned. When Daniel arrived, the king questioned Daniel, perhaps to make sure of his identity. He wanted to know if Daniel was one of the captives from Judah and if so, "you can give interpretations and explain enigmas." The king promised the great reward he had already promised the wise men if they could give an interpretation. The wise men were not able to do this, so the offer was made to Daniel (Daniel 5:13-16).

Daniel refused Belshazzar's gifts, but he was not disrespectful. Daniel was willing to explain the writing without a reward (Daniel 5:17).

5) Daniel reviewed the past. Daniel then began to review the past that led to the handwriting on the wall. God Most High had given Nebuchadnezzar the kingdom (Daniel 5:18). Because of this, Nebuchadnezzar had great power over the nations (Daniel 5:19). This power led to great pride in Nebuchadnezzar (Daniel 5:20). His pride led him to become like a beast, and he lost his throne and ate grass like oxen. This continued until "he knew that the Most High God rules in the kingdom of men, and appoints over it whomever He chooses" (Daniel 5:21).

We can envision Daniel pointing an accusing finger at Belshazzar and saying, "(Y)ou have not humbled your heart, although you knew all this" (Daniel 5:22). Daniel went on to say, "(Y)ou have lifted yourself up against the Lord of heaven." In his pride he had brought in the vessels from the temple in Jerusalem, and they had all drunk from them and praised their false gods and did not glorify "the God who holds your breath in His hand," Daniel reminded Belshazzar (Daniel 5:23). And then the fingers of the hand were sent from God and wrote the message on the wall (Daniel 5:24).

THE MESSAGE FROM THE LORD

Daniel read the inscription on the wall: "MENE, MENE, TEKEL, UPHARSIN" (Daniel 5:25). Daniel then began to give the interpretation of the words. MENE means "numbered." The repetition is for emphasis. The Lord had numbered Belshazzar's days. His time was up. "God has numbered your kingdom, and finished it" (Daniel 5:26).

TEKEL means "weighed." Belshazzar had been weighed in by the Lord's standards and had come up short. "You have been weighed in the balance, and found wanting" (Daniel 5:27).

UPHARSIN is the plural of PERES, which means divided. "Your kingdom has been divided and given to the Medes and Persians" (Daniel 5:28). Notice that the verbs in verse 28 are in the past tense. What the Lord has said and determined is an accomplished fact.

Belshazzar kept his word and rewarded Daniel for interpreting the handwriting on the wall. Then "that very night" (Daniel 5:30) the judgment of the Lord happened. Belshazzar was slain and "Darius the Mede received the kingdom." Scholars believe this was 539 BC. Darius was probably a governor appointed over Babylon until the son of Cyrus became co-ruler in 538 BC. Cyrus was the king of Persia and became the overall ruler of the region.

Herodotus, a Greek historian and the first to attempt to write a factual secular history, wrote about how Babylon was conquered. He wrote that Cyrus positioned his army at the points where the Euphrates River entered and exited the city. Another group dug a canal that diverted the river away from the city. When the water went down, the soldiers entered the city and captured it before anyone knew what had happened. Belshazzar and all the leaders of Babylon were involved in their drinking party.

LESSONS FROM THE HANDWRITING ON THE WALL

1) As believers, we know we live in a world flooded by a sensual, gluttonous, greedy, evil and unholy culture. We must stay faithful to the Lord in an ungodly world.

2) The Lord God is not finished with you. Daniel at this time was believed to be in his eighties. The Lord had kept him alive for such a moment as this. As long as you are alive, God has a plan and a purpose for you. Most of us have seen sporting events that were won at the last moment. The last batter hits a home run, a last second pass is caught for a touchdown, or a buzzer-beating shot wins the basketball game. As someone has said, "It's not over till it's over." Jesus said: "Be faithful until death, and I will give you the crown of life" (Revelation 2:101). Stay faithful to the end. Finish well.

3) This world will pass away. Just as Belshazzar lost his kingdom, one day we will die or Christ will come. So we should not strive for fame or fortune or power or prestige. Don't settle for temporary treasures. Look forward to the eternal home Jesus promised to His followers: "In My Father's house are many mansions ... I will come again and receive you to Myself ..." (John 14:2-3).

CHAPTER 6

THE LION KING
DANIEL 6:1-28

There was a Disney movie several years ago about lions entitled "The Lion King." The real Lion King is Jesus. "But one of the elders said to me, 'Do not weep! Behold, the Lion of the tribe of Judah, the Root of David, has prevailed to open the scroll and to loose its seven seals" (Revelation 5:5). Jesus was present with Daniel, and Daniel was not harmed by the lions. The events of Chapter 6 of Daniel revealed to the king of Babylon that the God of Daniel was the all-powerful God. "He delivers and rescues, and He works signs and wonders in heaven and earth, who has delivered Daniel from the power of the lions" (Daniel 6:27).

RECALLED TO SERVICE

At the end of Chapter 5, Babylon had been conquered by the Medes and the Persians. Darius the Mede was made ruler over Babylon. Darius began to organize his kingdom. He appointed 120 "satraps." They would have been leaders over their local district or area. Over them there were "three governors of whom Daniel was one" (Daniel 6:1-2). "Because an excellent spirit" was in Daniel, he was clearly seen to be superior to all the other leaders. So much so that the king thought about making Daniel the leader over all the rest (Daniel 6:3).

EVIL POLITICIANS

Just as it is true today, it was true then that there are politicians whose only goal is power, prestige, and prosperity. So the governors and satraps began an intense investigation to seek to uncover some fault in Daniel's work so that they might bring charges against him. They were unsuccessful because Daniel was faithful in his duties, and was serving with honesty and integrity (Daniel 6:4). Daniel's enemies realized that if some law of the land conflicted with "the law of his God" that could trap him (Daniel 6:5).

The governors and satraps devised an evil scheme. In a large group they came to the king (Daniel 6:6). They started their presentation with a lie as many politicians do. They stated that "all" the leaders in the whole kingdom that a "firm decree" should be established "that whoever petitions any god or man for thirty days except you, O king, shall be cast into the den of lions" (Daniel 6:7). The king was so flattered and prideful that he "signed the written decree" that he would be the only one worshiped for thirty days (Daniel 6:8). The "law of the Medes and Persians" (Daniel 6:8) signified a law that could not be revoked, even by the king. It would remain in force until its stated time of expiration.

DANIEL'S REACTION

When Daniel learned that the decree had been signed, he went home. Without any hesitation, he continued with his regular practice of praying three times a day by the windows of his house that faced toward Jerusalem.

Daniel continued to be faithful, fearless, and consistent in his devotion to the Lord. He kept on doing what he had always done. His enemies were correct in assuming that Daniel would choose to continue worshiping his God rather than to follow the decree to worship Darius, even if it meant his death (Daniel 6:10).

THE EVIL PLOT CARRIED OUT

The enemies of Daniel spied on him and found that Daniel was praying to his God and not the king (Daniel 6:11). They immediately went to the king and reminded him of his decree, and he acknowledged that what they said was true (Daniel 6:12). They declared that Daniel was guilty (Daniel 6:13). The king was "greatly displeased with himself" because he realized that he had been tricked into betraying a good man. He wanted to deliver Daniel and sought some loophole in the law (Daniel 6:14).

The group again approached the king and told him the law must be enforced. So the king commanded that the sentence be carried out. Daniel was arrested and cast into the den of lions. The Aramaic word for "den" means "pit." A stone was placed over the opening of the pit to ensure that no one could intervene to help Daniel. The stone was impressed with the royal seal and with the seals of all the king's lords (Daniel 6:16-17). The king, perhaps moved by compassion or hope, told Daniel: "Your God, whom you serve continually, He will deliver you" (Daniel 6:16). This is not a statement of faith by Darius because in the morning he called out to Daniel to see if the "living God" had delivered him (Daniel 6:20).

After Daniel had been thrown into the pit, the king returned to his palace. He refused to eat, refused the musicians who might comfort him, and could not sleep (Daniel 6:18). The lions wanted to eat but couldn't, and apparently they slept!

The king was up early and rushed to the pit and called out to Daniel (Daniel 6:19-20). Daniel was alive and responded, "O king live forever!" (Daniel 6:21). This is the standard greeting for the king. It is ironic that he would bless the king in that way. The only way Darius or anyone else will live forever is to trust Daniel's God, the Lord Jesus Christ, who is the source of eternal life — as is shown by Daniels's safety in the den with the lions.

Daniel then explained that God sent His angel and shut the lion's mouths because Daniel was innocent before God and the king (Daniel 6:22). Daniel was spared because he believed in "his God" (Daniel 6:23). Daniel's faithfulness got him into trouble, and his faith got him out of it. Daniel gave all the credit to God.

In the roll call of the faithful in the Book of Hebrews it notes those "who through faith subdued kingdoms, worked righteousness, obtained promises, stopped the mouths of lions ..." (Hebrews 13:33).

The King's Reaction

The king commanded that all those who had accused Daniel and their families be thrown into the pit of the lions (Daniel 6:24).

Then the king wrote a public decree that everyone should revere the God of Daniel because, "He is the living God ... . His kingdom ... shall endure to the end ... . He delivers and rescues ..." (Daniel 6:25-27).

What Can We Learn from this Powerful Event?

1) Like Daniel, we should have a deep commitment to the Lord. The only fault Daniel's enemies could find with him was Daniel's commitment to God. Have you really committed your time and resources to the Lord? If someone observed your life, would the only fault they would find in you be your love for Jesus?

2) Daniel's miraculous deliverance. Daniel was saved from the lions, but the greatest miracle in your life is when you are saved from your sins by God's grace through faith in Jesus. All that the Lord does for you by His power and love is a gift and we should praise and thank the Lord.

3) The lions are still here. Daniel was not saved from the pit full of lions, but in the pit full of lions! Today we are surrounded by lions of many sins and temptations. Peter wrote: "(B)ecause your adversary the devil walks about like a roaring lion, seeking whom he may devour" (1

Peter 5:8). The devil is only "like" a lion. The true "lion of the tribe of Judah" is Jesus Christ. The God who delivered Daniel is able to deliver you. You may not be saved from a situation, but the Lord is with you in that situation. Paul wrote: "But the Lord stood with me and strengthened me, so that the message might be preached fully through me, and that all the Gentiles might hear. Also I was delivered out of the mouth of the lion. And the Lord will deliver me from every evil work and preserve me for His heavenly kingdom" (2 Timothy 4:17-18).

4) *Daniel had a prayer plan.* Daniel had rather faced the lions than given up his time with the Lord. What about you? Do you have a prayer plan? Daniel's plan included an upper room in his home with the windows opened toward Jerusalem. He was on his knees, three times a day and gave thanks to the Lord (Daniel 6:10). You and I need a plan. It would involve a quiet place and a certain time. Prayer should be at the top of the list of things we do.

If someone were to observe your life, would the greatest fault they would discover in you would be your love for Jesus and the time you spent in prayer?

ANIMAL PLANET
DANIEL 7:1-14

A program that is popular on television is called "Animal Planet." Programs are presented of various animals from around the world. I thought that was an appropriate title for the first part of Daniel Chapter 7. Both in Daniel and the Book of Revelation, animals are used as images to describe truth. Even today, we use animals to describe human behavior. For example, a person might be described as being "as strong as an ox" or "as stubborn as a mule."Animals can give us a graphic picture of our behavior. Daniel's vision in Chapter 7 gave God's view of various pagan governments. In Chapter 7 Daniel's writing changes from biography and turns to prophecy. A series of visions are reported that occurred in the last twenty years of Daniel's life. The visions are about the nations, especially as they affect Israel.

The first and greatest vision is in Chapter 7 of Daniel. This is the most complete Old Testament prophecy of the future. Many Jewish scribes believed it is the most important chapter in the Old Testament. Jewish men were not allowed to read Daniel until they were grown.

THE VISION

1) The date. The time of the vision is given in verse 1: "In the first year of Belshazzar king of Babylon" (Daniel 7:1). Daniel's book is not in chronological order since Belshazzar's death is recorded in Chapter 5. Scholars believe the date is about 550 BC. This is the date for the establishment of the Medo-Persian Empire under Cyrus.

2) *Four winds, four beasts.* On that night as Daniel was in bed, he had a dream and visions came to him and he wrote them down (Daniel 7:1). In the vision Daniel saw "the four winds of heaven" stirred up the Great Sea or the Mediterranean Sea. Wind blowing from one direction can be strong, but imagine wind blowing from all four directions at one time (Daniel 7:2). Out of this stirred sea came four beasts (Daniel 7:3). Each of these beasts was different and represented kings (Daniel 7:17) or kingdoms (Daniel 7:18, 23).

3) *Daniel Chapter 2.* Nebuchadnezzar had a dream. A vast statue of a man was made up of four metals: a head of gold, a chest and arms of silver, thighs of bronze, legs of iron, and feet of mixed clay and iron. Daniel explained that the metal represented four world empires. These empires decreased in value but increased in strength. Nebuchadnezzar was the head of gold, the Medes and Persians were the chest and arms, the bronze thighs represented Greece, and the iron was Rome. The feet of iron and clay represented various countries at the end of time. The stone cut from the mountain that hit the feet represented Jesus Christ, who will come to destroy all human kingdoms and set up His kingdom. So how do these two dreams relate?

4) *The four beasts.* The churning sea may represent all of humanity. Out of this tumult of people come nations that are fighting for power and control. Out of this chaos four empires emerge. The first was a "lion, and had eagle's wings" (Daniel 7:4). The lion is considered to be the king of the beasts, and the eagle, the king of the birds. This description was of Nebuchadnezzar and the Babylonian Empire. Almost all scholars down through the years have agreed that the vision of Chapter 7 and that of

Chapter 2 are the same four kingdoms.

Archaeologists have found winged lions on statues and on wall reliefs and paintings on walls in the ruins of the old city of Babylon. The words "plucked off" (Daniel 7:4) is a reference to Nebuchadnezzar's humiliation (Daniel 4:28-33).

The next animal, representing the next empire, is "like a bear ... raised up on one side, and had three ribs in its mouth" (Daniel 7:5). The bear represents Babylon's successor, the Medo-Persian Empire (Daniel 2:38, 39). "Raised on one side" means that the Persians were the dominant partner over the Medes. The "three ribs" represent the three kingdoms that the Medo-Persians had conquered: Egypt, Lydia, and Babylon.

The "four-headed," "four-winged leopard" represents Greece (Daniel 7:6). Wings are a symbol for speed. Alexander the Great quickly conquered the whole area. The "leopard" represented power and speed. The four heads of the leopard describe the four "heads" of government which ruled after Alexander's death. Alexander's empire was divided into four parts among his generals, Macedonia, Egypt, Syria, and Thrace.

The fourth beast was "dreadful, terrible, and strong." It had "huge iron teeth" and destroyed all the nations that were before it (Daniel 7:7). This beast was not compared to any animal. The "huge iron teeth" probably refer to the "iron legions of Rome," a description of the Roman army with swords and shields of iron.

The ten horns represent powerful countries at the end of time related to that part of the world. The United States could possibly be in this picture because of its close relationship with the countries of Europe and the Middle East. The "little horn" with "eyes of a man" and speaking pompous words" probably represents the Antichrist (Daniel 7:7-8).

THE VISION OF HEAVEN

1) Daniel's vision then shifted to heaven. "Thrones" were arranged. Since "thrones" is plural, this is symbolic of the Almighty God, the Father; the Son of God, our Lord Jesus Christ; and the Holy Spirit (Daniel 7:9). The plural is seen in the very beginning: "Let us make man in our image" (Genesis 1:26). "And the Spirit of God was hovering over the face of the waters: (Genesis 1:2).

2) "Ancient of Days." This term is used to describe the eternal God. The phrase suggests age, dignity, endurance, judgment, and wisdom. This term clearly describes the Lord God revealed in the Bible. Later, "the One like the Son of Man" came to the Ancient of Days, and the Son of Man was given an "everlasting kingdom" (Daniel 7:13-14). This is clearly a portrayal of the return of our Lord Jesus Christ in glory.

3) The description. "His garment was white like snow," refers to purity. "Wash me and I shall be whiter than snow" (Psalm 51:7). White hair — "His head was like pure wool" describes wisdom. "(A)nd in the midst of the seven lampstands One like the Son of Man, clothed with a garment down to His feet and girded about the chest with a golden band. His head and hair were white like wool, as white as snow ..." (Revelation 1:13-14).

"His throne was a fiery flame" symbolizes that the Lord God is in control. The Lord is the one who executes judgment. The "wheels a burning fire" and a "fiery steam issued" continues the picture of the powerful judgment of God (Daniel 7:9-10). The power and judgment described as fire associated with God is a common idea in the Bible; for example, Exodus 3:2, Amos 5:6, Hebrews 12:29, and Revelation 20:9.

"Wheels a burning fire" refers to the chariot in which God rides to battle to demonstrate His sovereignty and execute judgment (compare Ezekiel 1:15-21, 10:1-22). In Ezekiel's vision in Chapter 1, the throne had wheels that could go in all directions at once. The "wheels" express the truth that the Lord God is not confined to one place. Whether it is heaven, or Jerusalem, or in a church, the Lord is present in all places, at all times.

THE MULTITUDES AT THE THRONE

1) *"A thousand thousands ... ten thousand times ten thousand"* (Daniel 7:10) refers to the immeasurable servants of God and is not meant to be a specific number. "After these things I looked, and behold, a great multitude, which no one could number ... standing before the throne and before the Lamb ... " (Revelation 7:9).

2) *Judgment was begun and the books were opened* (Daniel 7:10). The "books" record the names and works of those who will be judged. "And I saw the dead, small and great, standing before God, and books were opened. And another book was opened, which is the Book of Life" (Revelation 20:12). There is another comparison in the Book of Revelation: "But there shall by no means enter it anything that defiles, or causes an abomination or a lie, but only those who are written in the Lamb's Book of Life" (Revelation 21:27).

3) *The "horn" judged.* The Antichrist, the "horn" speaking "pompous words," was "slain" and given to the "burning flame" (Daniel 7:11). "The devil, who declined them, was cast into the lake of fire and brimstone ..." (Revelation 20:10). The "rest of the beasts" (Daniel 7:12), referring to the other nations "lost their dominion," but their "lives were prolonged for a season and a time." The "rest of the beasts" referred to Babylon, Medo-Persia, and Greece. Although these empires passed away, their "dominion" was passed on to their successors. "(A) season and a time" is an expression for an indefinite period of time. The focus of the vision is on the last days and the judgment of God on the nations.

CHRIST COMES

1) Son of Man. Verses 13 and 14 are a clear prophecy of the second coming of Christ. "One like the Son of Man" is a name that Jesus often called Himself: "But as the days of Noah were, so also will the coming of the Son of Man be" (Matthew 29:37). "… (I)n the midst of the seven lampstands One like the Son of Man" (Revelation 1:13). These are just two examples from the New Testament that clearly show that the name "Son of Man" is Jesus.

2) "Coming with the clouds." "They will see the Son of Man coming on the clouds of heaven" (Matthew 24:30). "Behold, He is coming with clouds …" (Revelation 1:7). These two references confirm Daniel's prophecy that the Coming One is Jesus. This is wonderful news for believers, but terrifying news for those who have rejected Jesus (Daniel 7:13).

3) "He came to the Ancient of Days." Jesus appeared in heaven before His Father for His coronation. Jesus was crowned King of kings and Lord of lords. Jesus was given "dominion" or authority, "glory" or praise, and the "kingdom" which is "everlasting." Jesus will reign over "all peoples, nations, and languages" (Daniel 7:14). "And He has on His robe and on His thigh a name written: King of kings and Lord of lords" (Revelation 19:16). All nations will serve Jesus. "And at the name of Jesus every knee shall bow of those in heaven, and those on earth, and of those under the earth" (Philippians 2:10).

4) "His dominion is an everlasting dominion." Christ's kingdom will "not pass away," and "shall not be destroyed." Jesus said: "I am the Alpha and the Omega, the Beginning and the End, says the Lord, who is and who was and who is to come, the Almighty" (Revelation 1:8).

LESSONS FROM THE VISION

1) Jesus the Son of Man and the Son of God is coming again. People say: "(W)here is the promise of His coming? All things continue as they have from the beginning of creation" (2 Peter 3:4). Jesus will come suddenly, unannounced like a "thief in the night" (Revelation 21:20; 2 Peter 3:10). Many will continue in their sin, not believing in Jesus Christ, but He will come and judge the world.

2) The judgment. Earthly kingdoms can be brutal and destructive, but even if they are good, they will all end. Nothing man-made lasts forever. Only what is done for Jesus will last. This is the history of humanity until Jesus comes. Then all earthly kingdoms are replaced by the kingdom of God and judgment comes.

3) The books are opened. The Lamb's Book of Life will be opened and all whose names are not in it will not enter the kingdom of God. On earth the only book that matters is the Bible. The Bible is the Word of God. The Bible teaches us about the Lord and His dealings with people through the years revealing His plan of salvation. The climax of God's plan was the first coming of the Lord Jesus Christ and the fulfillment of our redemption.

4) The Antichrist. The Antichrist, the "little horn" speaking "pompous words," will be slain and "given to the burning flame" (Daniel 7:11). "The devil, who deceived them, was cast into the lake of fire and brimstone where the beast and the false prophet are. And they will be tormented day and night forever and ever" (Revelation 20:10).

5) God is in control of history. History is moving towards God's conclusion. The Lord said: "Behold, I make all things new" (Revelation 24:5). "They need no lamp nor light of the sun, for the Lord God gives them light. And they shall reign forever and ever" (Revelation 22:5).

CHAPTER 8

THE BATTLE OF
THE BIG MOUTH LITTLE HORN
DANIEL 7:15-28

As I write this in August of 2021, there is total chaos in Afghanistan after the United States withdrew our military forces from the country, leaving American civilians, embassy personnel and billions of dollars of military equipment. In a matter of days, the terrorist groups of the Taliban, Al-Qaida, and Isis overran the country. Afghans who helped the United States for the last twenty years were also left behind. In the early days of these events, the one word that describes the situation is chaos!

The rise and fall of nations is the chaos that is inherent in our human system of government. When the vision recorded in Chapter 7 of Daniel was over, Daniel was "grieved in his spirit" and "troubled" (Daniel 7:15). Then Daniel approached "one of those who stood by," apparently an angel, and asked him what the vision meant (Daniel 7:16). So the angel summed up the vision. The four great beasts are four kings that arise on the earth. But in spite of all that happens, "the saints of the Most High shall receive the kingdom" (Daniel 7:17-18).

DANIEL WANTED MORE DETAIL

Daniel may have been pleased at how all this ended, but he wanted to understand more of what would happen at the end. He wanted to know about the fourth beast that "trampled the residue with its feet" (Daniel 7:19). He also wanted to know more about the ten horns and the "other horn" which spoke "pompous words" who "was greater than his fellows" (Daniel 7:20).

1) Daniel saw more. As Daniel watched, this last horn "was making war against the saints, and prevailing against them" (Daniel 7:21). "Saints" means "holy ones" or people who have been separated from the world and are serving the Lord. The saints endured hardship and persecution until the Ancient of Days came and judged in favor of the saints and they received the kingdom (Daniel 7:22).

The kingdom possessed by the saints is the same everlasting kingdom ruled over by the Son of Man (Daniel 7:14). The Son of Man rules through His saints. "And he who overcomes, and keeps My works until the end, to him I will give power over the nations" (Revelation 2:26).

2) Daniel heard more. The angel then told Daniel: "The fourth beast shall be a fourth kingdom on earth ..." (Daniel 7:23), which is the Roman Empire. The "ten horns" are ten future kingdoms at the end of times (Daniel 7:24). "And another shall rise after them, "refers to the "little horn" (Daniel 7:8). This king will subdue three kings; blaspheme God, "speak pompous words against the Most High"; "persecute the saints" (Daniel 7:21, Revelation 13:7); "And shall intend to change times and the law" — and will dominate the saints for a brief period — "a time and times and half a time" (Daniel 7:25).

The dominion of the little horn will end when the court of God is convened and the kingdom of the little horn will be destroyed forever (Daniel 7:26). Then all the "kingdoms under the whole heaven" will be given to "the saints of the Most High." The kingdom of the Most High is everlasting and everyone will "serve and obey Him" (Daniel 7:27).

At the end of the angel's account, Daniel was "troubled" and kept all these things to himself (Daniel 7:28).

WHAT DOES THIS MEAN?

1) The biblical view. The first thing that we need to understand is that the Bible looks at history from the standpoint of God's people, Israel. Empires that don't involve Israel are not mentioned, although they may have been important.

2) The ten kings. The ten kings represent ten nations that in some way are connected to the Roman Empire. These nations exist at the end of time. The one ruler that will arise and be dominant (Daniel 7:24) is the "little horn" or "antichrist." Daniel Chapter 7 is the first extended revelation of the antichrist. There are further revelations in the New Testament in Matthew 24, 2 Thessalonians 2, and Revelation 13-19.

The Antichrist will attack believers and blaspheme God. In recent years the murder of thousands of believers has been common in Iraq. Franklin Graham reported that in 2016 there were 90,000 believers who had been killed around the world.

3) "Change times and the times." This does not mean to change the time of day, but to change the times symbolically. We speak of the "time in which we live" or of "changing times." Think about the things that are changing with the laws of God now. Marriage has been redefined. It is no longer one man and one woman, but it can be any number, or whoever, whatever. You don't have to live by your birth gender today. The medical forms you fill out have "male, female, other." Under the heading of "woman's choice," millions of defenseless unborn babies have been murdered. These are already antichrists in the world and the final one is coming soon.

4) The great battle. The Ancient of Days will come with judgment

(Daniel 7:22). The dominion of the Antichrist will be destroyed forever (Daniel 7:26). There will be a final battle won by Jesus Christ (Revelation 19: 19-21). Jesus will come on a white horse (Revelation 19:11). Out of His mouth will be a "sharp sword that with it He should strike the nations" (Revelation 19:15). The name "King of kings and Lord of lords" is written on His robe and His thigh (Revelation 19:16).

The beast, the kings of the earth and their armies "make war against Him who sat on the horse" (Revelation 19:20). Instantly the battle is over, the beast was captured and the false prophet. They were cast into the lake of fire (Revelation 19:20). This is the final destination of the little horn with the big mouth. The title of this chapter is "The Battle of the Big Mouth Little Horn." The battle is called the "battle of Armageddon" (Revelation 16:14-16). "... (T)o gather them to the battle of that great day of God Almighty ... (a)nd they gathered them together to the place called in Hebrew, Armageddon."

I believe that the Lord gave Daniel this vision in his day to encourage him, and through him, all Israel. The promise of the Lord is no matter how dark the times, the Lord God will be victorious. I believe the Lord gave John his revelation in his day to strengthen him in his imprisonment on the Isle of Patmos and to encourage the early church in dark times that the Lord Jesus will be victorious!

These two books, Daniel and Revelation have come down through the centuries for us today. The Word of God encourages us that no matter how dark our times, the Lord Jesus will be victorious, and we will dwell with Him in glory forever. Hallelujah!

BACK TO THE FUTURE

In order to see into the future, we need to go back about 2,600 years to Daniel. We need to go back to understand the future. Much of Daniel's vision has been fulfilled. The kingdoms of Babylon, the Medes and Persians, Greece, and Rome have come and gone. The truth of this prophecy should give us confidence that the rest of Daniel's vision will someday be fulfilled. So what should we be looking for near the end of the age? There are at least five things we need to watch for emanating from Daniel Chapter 7.

1) The rise in false spiritual authorities. There are many strange religions with people worshipping "wokeism," climate change, themselves, sex, money and drugs. Jesus warned: "Take heed that no one deceives you. For many will come in My name, saying 'I am the Christ,' and will deceive many" (Matthew 24:4-5). "Then many false prophets will rise up and deceive many" (Matthew 24:11). We must be vigilant and pray for discernment to see through the deceptions of the devil.

2) The rise of a powerful leader. In the midst of all of this chaos, people will desire a leader that can bring the world together. The "little horn" of Daniel will unite nations against God's people. He will attack the saints. There has been a movement for many years to establish international law. At some point there will be a desire to have a leader to lead in the enforcement of those laws. We have seen with the COVID pandemic that Americans have been forced to give up some of their individual freedoms in order to fight the pandemic. Because of the threat of nuclear weapons and terrorism, and the resulting chaos, Americans and others will give up their rights to be protected.

3) The rise of violence. Each beast in Daniel is more violent than the one before. It is written of the second beast, "Arise, devour much flesh" (Daniel 7:5). The fourth beast "was devouring ... breaking in pieces" (Daniel 7:7). The little horn was making war against the saints (Daniel 7:21). This rising violence is a part of the chaos at the end times.

4) The rise of hostility to Christians. The little horn was making war against the saints or the people of God. Islamic terrorists have killed Christians in Iraq, Syria, Libya, and Afghanistan. Thousands of Christians are slain around the world every year. Jesus said there will be "wars and rumors of wars" (Matthew 24:6). China has the largest military in the world and is threatening Taiwan. North Korea and Iran are testing long range missiles. Iran is not only a major sponsor of terrorist organizations, but they are also developing nuclear capability. The goal of radical Islam is to rule the world. Here in August of 2021, Afghanistan has fallen to the Taliban and our southern border is wide open. It could be all too easy for terrorists to enter the United States.

In the midst of all the chaos that may happen to us, we need to look to Jesus. "… (L)ooking unto Jesus, the author and finisher of our faith" (Hebrews 12:2). There is great encouragement in the second chapter of Daniel when the stone smashed the statue. That stone is the Lord Jesus Christ, the Rock of Ages, the stone of stumbling to unbelievers and the Rock of our salvation. Jesus is the stone the builders rejected, but He has become the chief cornerstone (Matthew 21:42). "The Lord is my rock and my fortress and my deliverer" (2 Samuel 22:2).

Build your life on the Rock of God's salvation, the Lord Jesus Christ. Stand on the Rock and on the last day you will still be standing when everything else has disappeared!

CHAPTER 9

THE RAM AND THE GOAT
DANIEL 8: 1-8

The vision in Daniel Chapter 8 occurred before the events in Chapter 5. The vision came to Daniel in "the third year of the reign of King Belshazzar" (Daniel 8:1). The event of the "Hand writing on the wall" occurred on the last day of Belshazzar's reign.

HANDWRITING ON THE WALL

When Belshazzar had his party and gathered all his nobles and their wives and concubines for a feast, he issued an order to bring the temple vessels captured in Jerusalem by Nebuchadnezzar's army. They began to drink from the vessels. What blasphemy! Suddenly the portion of a man's hand appeared and began to write on the wall. No one could understand the message until Daniel was called. Daniel understood and gave a clear message to the king and his nobles. The Babylonian Empire would fall and the kingdom would be ruled by the Medes and the Persians.

Now why was Daniel so sure what was going to happen in the future? Here in Chapter 9, Daniel revealed that he had previously had a vision from the Lord about what was going to happen.

THE VISION

God revealed that although He had a special relationship with Israel, there would be a period of Gentile domination because of Israel's sin. God was not casting them off permanently, but God was using the captivity as a penalty for their sin and to discipline His people. This vision would help Daniel to understand history and how the Gentiles would affect Israel. Remember, this vision occurred before the events in Chapter 5.

Since Abraham's time, the area of Israel has been the news center of the world. Events that have happened there have affected world history. Various nations have fought over this area. That part of the world is almost constantly in the news. Of course, Israel was the place of Jesus' birth. One day peace will reign there, but now it is the epicenter of strife, terrorism, and struggle.

GOD'S WORD IS TRUE

The truth of this vision encourages us about the truth of God's Word. Now some of the prophecies in the eighth chapter of Daniel have been fulfilled. But in Daniel's day all of the vision was in the future. We should be amazed at the truth of this vision and the power of the Lord who revealed it to Daniel.

1) The ram. Daniel gave the location of the vision as Shushan in the province of Elam by the River Ulai (Daniel 8:2). Shushan was about 230 miles east of Babylon. Ulai was a canal located a few miles from Shushan. Shushan would later become the capital of Persia. Shushan is the Hebrew word for Susa. At this time it was a small village in the desert. In his vision, Daniel was standing by this canal, and he saw a ram with two horns (Daniel 8:3). It is common for a ram to have two horns, but the second horn that came out was larger than the first (Daniel 8:3). In verse 20, the ram is identified with the Medes and the Persians.

Although the Medes came first, the Persians became dominant and absorbed the Medes, and it soon became the Persian Empire.

The Persian army wore on their garments and their shields a representation of a ram's head. They had poles topped with a replica of a ram's head. The Persians developed the Zodiac, and a ram's head has always been associated with Persia. It has also been associated today with the occult, horoscopes, and Satan worship.

The ram pushed to the west, the north, and the south conquering all it encountered. Cyrus controlled Babylon in the east, went north to the Caspian Sea, west into Syria and Asia Minor, and he went south into Egypt and Ethiopia. It was the largest empire the world had known up to that time (Daniel 8:4). The last part of verse 4 declares: "(H)e did according to his will and became great!" Cyrus pleased himself and made himself great. That's what power and pride can do. Boasting about our accomplishments is the temptation that comes with success and prosperity. All of this would come later. At the time of the vision, Persia was a little city state out in the desert.

2) The goat. The next animal was a male goat (Daniel 8:5). In Hebrew the word is "he-goat," that was symbolic of a chief or a leader. The goat was more powerful than the ram. The goat represented Greece (Daniel 8:21). The "notable horn" represented Alexander the Great (Daniel 8:21). "Without touching the ground" (Daniel 8:5) was the rapid conquest by Alexander. The goat attacked the ram and defeated it (Daniel 8:6-7).

After expanding the kingdom, the "large horn" was broken and "four notable ones came" (Daniel 8:8). Alexander the Great died at age thirty-three. After his death, four of his generals divided up the kingdom.

3) The little horn. This "little horn" is not the same as the "little horn" of Chapter 7. The little horn of Chapter 7 came out of Rome; this one came from Greece. This "little horn" probably refers to Antiochus

Epiphanes, the eighth king of the Syrian kingdom that ruled from 175 to 164 BC. This prophecy skips over 300 years from the time of Alexander to 175 BC and the time of Antiochus (Daniel 8:9). Antiochus invaded Egypt to the south, east is Parthia, and "the Glorious Land" is Palestine (Daniel 8:9-10). "He even exalted himself as high as the Prince of the host" (Daniel 8:11). He exalted himself as high as God! He would disrupt the daily sacrifices in the temple in Jerusalem and "cast truth down to the ground" (Daniel 8:11-12). The "truth" probably referred to the law of Moses.

Then a "holy one" asked, "How long will the vision be ... ?" (Daniel 8:13). The time, "two thousand three hundred days," refers to the time between Antiochus' pollution of the temple and the Maccabees' cleansing of the temple.

4) The legend. There is a legend that Greece was started by a group of people who were told to follow a goat and it would lead them to a place to settle. The story goes that the goat led them to a place they named "Goat City." The sea there, they named the "Aegean Sea," or "Goat Sea." So the goat is the representation of Greece. Daniel saw this as a vision 200 years before it happened.

Powerful Lessons

1) The Lord knows the future. The Lord not only knows the future, but He is the Lord who controls the future. Many things happen that make no sense to us, but we can be assured that the Lord is at work to complete His plan. The Lord is not concerned about the "little horn" because He will dehorn the Antichrist when the time comes.

2) Our trust must not be in this world. It is all right to have a career and be a patriotic American, because these things are not bad. But we cannot trust in things. Don't tie your eternal destiny to your job or your career. The kingdoms of this world and the companies of this world come and go, rise and fall. Don't be in love with this world. Your love should be focused on the Lord Jesus Christ. The prophet Jeremiah wrote "the Lord appeared of old to me, saying: 'Yes. I have loved you with an everlasting love, therefore with lovingkindness I have drawn you" (Jeremiah 31:3). Don't mistake the world's love with God's for Jesus died for our sins and His resurrection is a guarantee of eternal life to all believers.

3) The power of encouragement. Alexander the Great conquered the world in twelve years and never lost a battle. Historians believe that one reason for his success was the encouragement of his parents. Philip of Macedon, Alexander's father, ruled Macedonia, as Greece was called then. His career began by trying to drive the Persians from Macedonia. It is said that he told Alexander, "This place is too small for you, you need to seek out a kingdom worthy of yourself." As the legend goes, he was encouraged by his parents.

As believers in Jesus, we need to encourage our children to attempt great things for the Lord, to be willing to accept whatever challenge the Lord calls them to face. Knowing like Paul, "I can do all things through Christ who strengthens me" (Philippians 4:13).

4) Give God the glory. Alexander had a fatal flaw: his pride. He "grew very great" and "made himself great" (Daniel 8:8). He shined the light on himself. The American Standard Version of the Bible translated it like this: "(H)e magnified himself exceedingly." At the apex of his career he died at age thirty-two or thirty-three. He was despondent, depressed, and an alcoholic. He was sad because, "There were no more worlds to conquer." The world he never conquered was himself. He could conquer nations, but he could not conquer himself. What about you?

Many face this danger today. We have tremendous technology at our disposal, we have great luxury here in the United States, and we have education and great resources, but we cannot master ourselves. The only way you can master yourself is to surrender control of your heart and life to Jesus Christ. We need to be strong in the Lord. You and I will never be able to conquer our sin without faith in the Lord Jesus Christ. Alexander the Great was an important figure in history, but on a personal level, he was a loser.

5) *God's plan.* When Alexander conquered the world, he spread Greek culture, Greek language, and Greek roads all over the kingdom. A group of rabbis in Alexandria, Egypt translated the Hebrew scriptures from Hebrew into Greek, the common language. Later, the New Testament was written in Greek and the Greek-Roman roads became the highway for missionaries to carry the gospel and the Scriptures all over that part of the world. In God's plan, Alexander's work was a part of what God was doing in the world. God is in control of history. He is in control of your history, and He will bring history to His conclusion.

6) *The visions of Daniel.* The visions in the Book of Daniel have the unique purpose of revealing the Antichrist. We are warned that there are many antichrists in the world already (1 John 2:18). Their seductive purpose is to tempt you into the path of being an evil, deceptive person. He will become ruler of the world and declare himself to be god and force people to worship him (Revelation 13:12-17). For Daniel, Alexander was a prototype of the military side of the Antichrist.

7) *A call to courage in chaos.* I believe in the rapture of the church before the great tribulation. Only the Lord knows when all these end time events will happen. Our challenge as we live in this present evil age is to remain courageously faithful to the Lord Jesus Christ, our soon coming King.

In these chaotic times, we should maintain a steadfast faith in the Word of God that invites us: "Come unto Me all you who labor and are heavy laden and I will give you rest ..." (Matthew 11:28). Our world today is not only frightening, it is wearisome. Jesus will give you rest and peace.

Jesus is calling you today to stand on His Word, to stand on His promises to you. Jesus is in control of history, and He is in control of your personal history. Jesus said: "I go to prepare a place for you. And if I go and prepare a place for you, I will come again and receive you to Myself" (John 14:2-3).

CHAPTER 10

The Madman

DANIEL 8:9-11

Our chaotic world is fast becoming a madhouse. Hollywood's lack of morals has become common across America. Critical race theory is being taught in our schools, which is really teaching people of different races to distrust and hate one another. The rise of crime is startling. Our society is driven by lust, greed, and a desire for power. Historically, such conditions bring on a dictator. The last dictator to come will be the Antichrist, now awaiting his opportunity to make his appearance.

THE POWER OF THE ANTICHRIST

Alexander the Great was a type of military antichrist. The Antichrist at the end of time will come empowered by the demonic power of Satan. Jesus warned, "For false christs and false prophets will rise and show great signs and wonders to deceive, if possible, even the elect" (Matthew 24:24). And Paul explained: "The coming of the lawless one is according to the working of Satan, with all power, signs, and lying wonders, and with all unrighteous deception among those who perish, because they did not receive the love of the truth, that they might be saved" (2 Thessalonians 2:9-10).

This description of the evil antichrist — and the desecration of the temple in Jerusalem and stopping the sacrifices (Daniel 8:11-12) — has led most commentators to pinpoint another man as a type of antichrist, Antiochus II.

ANTIOCHUS

Antiochus was eighth in a line of twenty-six kings who ruled over the Syrian kingdom. The area included Israel, Gaza, Lebanon, Jordan, and Syria. This was one of four sections of Alexander's Empire. Antiochus named himself "Epiphanes" or "God manifest" and had that stamped on his coins. The common people nicknamed him "Epimanes" or "madman."

1) Antiochus persecuted the Jews. He cruelly persecuted the Jews just as the Antichrist will do at the end of time. He attacked Israel, thinking they were in revolt and killed 40,000 men, women, and children. Many thousands were sold into slavery.

2) Antiochus hated God's truth. He banned the possession of and the reading of the Hebrew Scriptures. He made it illegal to circumcise their sons and to observe holy days. He polluted the temple in Jerusalem by sacrificing pigs on the altar. He ordered pig blood to be put on all the items of the temple. Antiochus tore down the curtain of the Holy of Holies and poured pig blood on everything. He placed a statue of Zeus in the temple. Antiochus' wickedness is a picture of the wicked nature of the Antichrist.

3) Antiochus' death. The Jews revolted and recaptured Jerusalem and cleansed the temple. Antiochus was enraged and swore to make Jerusalem the Jews' burial ground. But he was struck by an incurable disease and died in horrible pain.

4) Antiochus, a type of antichrist. Both were called a "little horn." Antiochus was called a little horn: "And out of one of them came a little horn …" (Daniel 8:9). And it was written of the Antichrist as a little horn: "I was considering the horns, and there was a horn, a little one, coming up among them ... and a mouth speaking pompous words" (Daniel 7:8).

Both are judged by the Lord. Antiochus died a painful death, and the Antichrist will be cast into the lake of fire: "These two were cast alive into the lake of fire ..." (Revelation 19:20). Antiochus is a picture of the "lawless one" to come. He was arrogant and evil, as seen by his naming of himself "Epiphanes," "God Manifest."

5) Similarities today. Antiochus polluted the temple in Jerusalem. There were two different Jewish temples that together stood for about 900 years. The first was Solomon's temple that was destroyed by the Babylonians. The second one was Herod's temple that was leveled by the Romans in AD 70. The site of the temple is mentioned 400 times in the Bible. Yet a few years ago, the United Nations voted to deny all Jewish ties to the temple mound. The Dome of the Rock Mosque is located on the temple mound. The United Nations denied any Jewish or Christian connection to the temple area and accused Israel of endangering this holy site. There is also a growing anti-Israel sentiment in the United States. There have been public physical attacks on Jews in the streets of some of our major cities in the summer of 2021.

God's plan is for the salvation of the Jews: "And they also, if they do not continue in unbelief, will be grafted in, for God is able to graft them in again" (Romans 11:23). So it is not too late for Israel to repent and accept their Messiah, Jesus Christ. Our salvation was made when we were grafted in: "(Y)ou, being a wild olive tree, were grafted in among them, and with them became a partaker of the root and fatness of the olive tree ..." (Romans 11:17).

It is important for believers to be steadfast and faithful to the Lord Jesus Christ in these chaotic times. As these things unfold, the return of our Lord Jesus seems near at hand.

THE HAMMER

1) In Daniel's vision, two angels were talking, and one said: "How long will the vision be ... ?" (Daniel 8:13). The answer was "two thousand three hundred days" (Daniel 8:14). From the time that Antiochus began to persecute the Jews until his death was 2,300 days! The word of God is true. Some Bible scholars think that the number applies to the period of the Great Tribulation at the end of time.

2) Mattathias. Another person that appeared in history between the close of the Old Testament and before New Testament times was a man named Mattathias. He was an elderly priest of the Jews who lived in a village outside Jerusalem. When Antiochus began a persecution of his village, Mattathias refused to bow down to the Greek gods. He began a revolution. After his death, his son Judas became the leader of the revolt. He was named "Maccabees" or "Hammer." Judas and his followers recaptured Jerusalem and cleansed the temple. One of the things they needed to do was burn oil in the temple for eight days, but they could only find one container of holy oil. Yet it lasted eight days! The Jews rejoiced and celebrated the dedication of the temple and call it to this day "Hanukkah." Hanukkah is celebrated during our Christmas celebration.

3) The Lord delivers. We know that the greatest deliverance of the Lord happened on the cross when Jesus died for sin, was buried and rose again. Looking back through the Old Testament there are many times when the Lord delivered His people. Pharaoh tried to destroy the Jews, but God delivered them from Pharaoh through the Red Sea. The freedom from Egypt is celebrated in the Passover. When Haman sought to destroy the Jews, Esther intervened, and God delivered. The Jews celebrate this week by celebrating the Feast of Purim. Antiochus sought to destroy the Jews, but God delivered them, and the Jews mark this event with the Feast of Dedication. Satan tried to destroy Jesus, but

Jesus arose from the tomb. We, believers, celebrate this greatest of all deliverances with Easter!

When you face personal times of difficulty or trials or persecution, you can rejoice in the fact God is going to deliver you and the result will be a celebration. If you are facing difficult times right now know that Jesus is King and Lord over all. He will deliver in His time and in His way.

WHAT DOES THIS MEAN FOR YOU TODAY

1) Our hearts should be compassionate for others. We may know little or nothing about what other hurts people have, but we should show compassion on them. Daniel learned a little portion of God's plan and he wondered when it all would end. Today, we have a more complete idea of God's plan for everybody in the whole world. Yet today, many sit comfortably in their church pews with the Bible blahs, refusing to leave their comfort zones and join Jesus in seeking and saving the lost. Are these people really saved? That's not my judgment call. But the judgment of the Lord is coming. "For we shall all stand before the judgment seat of Christ.... So each of us shall give account of himself to God" (Romans 14:10, 12).

Our hearts should be moved with compassion for our relatives, friends, and others who are lost without Jesus Christ.

2) Take the Word of God seriously. We must realize that the Lord has a plan for each of us. We should not ignore or compromise His Word. His Word is true, and we should not marginalize or disobey His Word, but read it, pray over it, and obey it. The Lord delivered His Word to Daniel through dreams and visions. We have God's written Word, the Bible. Make the Bible your guide for life.

3) Face the challenge. There have been madmen in the past, and there will be madmen in the future. There will also be people of faith in the Lord Jesus who will have the courage to stand up for Jesus. Will you be one of them? Will you be like Daniel? Will you stand in your faith looking forward to the coming of the Lord Jesus Christ? Jesus is coming for believers. Is He coming for you?

CHAPTER 11

SATAN'S SUPER VILLAIN
DANIEL 8:15-27

A study of the End Times can be very confusing. Almost every Bible teacher or commentary has an opinion or a theory about how things will work out that vary from one to the other. No one has all the answers, but the Lord. A good starting place for our understanding is to learn what light the Book of Daniel sheds on the End Times. First, there was the appearance of Gabriel.

GABRIEL

1) Daniel was seeking the meaning of the vision when "one having the appearance of a man" stood before him (Daniel 8:15). The Hebrew word for a dream or a vision comes from the Hebrew word "to see." God used dreams and visions as a means of revelation to His people. Daniel received a message through a vision about the future, and Daniel needed help to understand the vision. Without the revelation of the Lord in the Scripture people have no hope.

2) The voice. The voice spoke and said: "Gabriel, make this man understand the vision" (Daniel 8:16). When Jesus was baptized by John in the Jordan River, a dove descended upon Jesus, and "a voice from heaven saying, "This is My beloved Son, in whom I am well pleased"

(Matthew 3:17). Jesus invited Peter, James, and John to accompany Him up a mountain. While they were there, Jesus was transfigured with brilliant light. Moses and Elijah appeared to them and "behold, a bright cloud overshadowed them; and suddenly a voice came out of the cloud saying, "This is My beloved Son, in whom I am well pleased. Hear Him!" (Matthew 17:1-5). This must certainly be the voice of God who spoke to Gabriel.

One of the tasks of angels is to be God's messengers. Gabriel is mentioned twice in Luke (Luke 1:19, 26), when he announced the births of John the Baptist and Jesus.

3) *When Gabriel came near to Daniel,* Daniel fell on his face because he was so afraid (Daniel 8:17). Gabriel began to explain that the vision "refers to the time of the end" (Daniel 8:17). Daniel was so frightened that he was in a "deep sleep," but Gabriel touched him and stood him upright (Daniel 8:18). Gabriel began his explanation by revealing that the vision was for at the "appointed time the end shall be" (Daniel 8:19). The two horns are the Medes and the Persians. The male goat is Greece and after the first king will come four kingdoms (Daniel 8:20-22).

4) *The Antichrist revealed.* "And in the latter time of their kingdom" refers to the end of Greek rule (Daniel 8:23). "When transgressors have reached their fullness ..." (Daniel 8:23) means when the sinful actions of the Jews have come to the point where God will bring His judgment upon them. "A king shall arise" probably referred to Antiochus, the king of Syria. "Not by his own power" means that Antiochus would be empowered by Satan. He would be ruthless, destructive, and deceptive (Daniel 8:24-25). Antiochus will exalt himself and "even rise against the Prince of princes" (Daniel 8:25).

Daniel was then told to seal up the vision. Documents were written on scrolls that could be rolled up and sealed to protect them. Daniel was sickened by the vision for days (Daniel 8:26-27).

5) *Antiochus was a type of antichrist.* When the Antichrist comes, the world will be in a terrible moral condition. What about now? For so many, lying has become the national pastime. Hollywood morals or no morals have become Main Street U.S.A. morals. This world is ready for the Antichrist now. Even many in the church are caught up in this worldly lack of morals. "Let no one deceive you by any means; for that Day will not come unless the falling away comes first ..." (2 Thessalonians 2:3). Many people today have departed from the truth of God's Word. Many people today don't believe in the miracles of the Bible, or the virgin birth of Jesus or His resurrection from the dead. Many who claim to be Christians think adultery is OK, and murder by abortion is OK, and the list goes on.

6) *Why not now?* "And now you know what is restraining, that he may be revealed in his own time .... He who restrains will do so until He is taken out of the way." The restrainer, the Holy Spirit, had to be taken out of the world so the Antichrist would be revealed. God has restrained sin through the power of the Holy Spirit. The Spirit uses the Bible, believers, and angels to restrain evil and proclaim the Kingdom of God. "Taken out of the way" may refer to the Rapture of the church. The church cannot exist without the Holy Spirit. The removal of the church would mean the removal of restraint on the power of sin.

THE DESCRIPTION OF SATAN'S SUPER VILLAIN

The angel Gabriel gave a vivid description of the Antichrist. This super villain will have "fierce features," use "sinister schemes" (Daniel 8:23), have "power," be "destructive" (Daniel 8:24), be "cunning," "deceitful," "exalt himself," and "rise against the Prince of princes" (Daniel 8:25). The result of all these characteristics is not victory, but defeat: "He shall be broken."

The world will look for some leader to bring prosperity, safety and peace out of world chaos. Through his cunning and deceitfulness, he will fool people as the world moves closer to one world ruler, one world government, and one world religion.

1) *The plot.* Satan's super villain will attack the people of God. "He shall destroy the mighty, and also the holy people" (Daniel 8:24c). But remember, the spirit of the Antichrist is already at work in the world. Christians today are being labeled as intolerant, bigots, and racists. Some in our government have recently stated that America's greatest threat is from white, male Christians. Believers are being portrayed as the enemy. We are told that we need a "green new deal" to save the environment, but that the murder of millions of innocent unborn children is all right. You are called racists if you question any of the decisions of the radical socialists in the United States today. We are being told that religion has no place in politics. Our nation seems to be moving toward making Bible-believing Christianity illegal! In some states, many churches were forced to close during the pandemic.

2) *Attack the Prince.* "He shall even rise against the Prince of princes" (Daniel 8:25c). Satan's super villain will attack the truth of the Scriptures, believers, and the holiness of our Lord Jesus Himself. Already, there is an effort to remove any sign of our Christian heritage from our history books. My wife and I visited Jamestown, Virginia, one year, and we noticed that the walls of only one structure remained. It was the ruins of a church and in the yard of the church was a statue commemorating the first pastor. Our early historical documents are filled with references to God. Yet, today there are some who want to remove the phrase "One Nation Under God" from the pledge of allegiance to the flag of the United States. Some want to remove "In God We Trust" from our coins and from our public buildings.

3) *The end of Satan's super villain.* His end will be sudden. "Broken without human means" (Daniel 8:25c). His kingdom will be destroyed

by the coming of the King of kings and the Lord of lords! (Revelation 19:20).

You may wonder, what has all this to do with me? The answer is that Jesus is coming for believers and then the world will be in a time of trouble and tribulation that has never been experienced before. What will happen to you will depend on what you do about having a relationship with Jesus Christ. Commit your heart and life to Jesus now if you have not already done so. Invite others to join you in following Jesus before it is too late. Where will you be when the super villain takes over the world?

When Daniel realized the meaning of the vision, he was "sick for days" (Daniel 8:27). What effect do these words have on your heart? I pray that these words will move you to repentance and faith in the Lord Jesus Christ.

CHAPTER 12

WHERE POWERFUL PRAYER BEGINS
DANIEL 9:1-3

We may all have a different opinion about where and how powerful prayer begins. We can see clearly from Daniel that his powerful prayer began with confession. The promise, "The effective, fervent prayer of righteous man avails much," is often quoted to encourage people to pray earnestly (James 5:16). But you may have forgotten that the first half of that verse is: "Confess your sins to one another and pray for one another, that you may be healed." Prayers that are powerful and effective involve mutual confession among believers. When we confess our sin to the Lord and stop playing religious games and ask the Lord and others we have offended for forgiveness, then our prayers are effective. This truth is essential to understand the ninth chapter of Daniel. Daniel's prayer is a long confession of the sins of Israel.

The confession of our sin should not be a rare experience. We should live a life of repentance, being confessed up-to-date with the Lord! We should be humbled by knowing that we are nothing without the Lord. Left to ourselves we are sheep always going astray.

DANIEL AND PRAYER

Daniel did not teach us about prayer by giving us rules or laws. He taught by example. Read through Daniel Chapter 9 and then read Jesus' model prayer in Matthew 6:5-15. You will notice some similarities that Daniel revealed out of his experience and that Jesus taught us in His model prayer.

1) The prior event. Daniel's motivation to pray was brought on by the vision recorded in Chapter 8. As the vision projected the future, it included future suffering that matches what occurred under Antiochus Epiphanes. He claimed to be "God manifest" and persecuted the Jews. Antiochus was a prototype of the coming end times Antichrist. For a man of faith like Daniel, the obvious thing to do when he learned the prophecy of coming suffering and sorrow was to call out to God in prayer.

2) The time of the prayer. The prayer was made in the "first year of Darius the son of Ahasuerus" (Daniel 9:1). That would have been the same time period of the sixth chapter of Daniel. Remember the sixth chapter was about Daniel's experience of being thrown into the lion's den. The word, "Darius," was a title. The word meant "holder of the scepter." The first year of Darius was 539 BC. "Darius" was a royal title and could have meant Cyrus or someone he appointed over Babylon. Daniel had come to Babylon as a youth in 605 BC and at this point was about eighty years old. Israel had been in captivity for about sixty-five years.

3) The books. In verse 2 Daniel was looking at the "books" or "scrolls" of the Bible. By Daniel's time a great part of what we call the Old Testament had been written. He could have scrolls of the Law; the first five books of Moses; the history books and Psalms and Proverbs. Daniel also had a scroll of the writings of Jeremiah. So one prophet was reading another prophet's scroll.

Daniel was a faithful follower of God. Daniel prayed, God delivered him from the lion's den, he received revelations from the Lord, he interpreted other people's dreams, yet he was a man who had a need to read the Word of God! If a man of faith like Daniel felt that need, how much more should we be studying the Word of God.

4) *Jeremiah's prophecy.* The prophecy was that the "desolations of Jerusalem" would last seventy years (Daniel 9:2). There are two places Daniel might have been reading: Jeremiah 25:11: "And this whole land shall be a desolation and an astonishment, and these nations shall serve the king of Babylon seventy years; or Jeremiah 29:10: "For thus says the Lord: After seventy years are completed at Babylon, I will visit you and perform My good word toward you, and cause you to return to this place." God had some good words for them. The words were "hope," "peace" and "future": "For I know the thoughts that I think toward you, says the Lord, thoughts of peace and not of evil, to give you a future and a hope" (Jeremiah 29:11). The Lord promised, "I will bring you back from your captivity ..." (Jeremiah 29:14).

When Daniel read these words from the scroll of Jeremiah, what did he do? Did he preach it? Did he share it? Did he tell it to others? No, Daniel prayed!

5) *How Daniel prayed.* "Then I set my face toward the Lord God ..." (Daniel 9:3). Daniel put his focus on the Lord. We also are challenged: "... looking unto Jesus, the author and finisher of our faith ..." (Hebrews 12:2). Just like Daniel, our focus, our heart should be on the Lord. That is why it is so important to understand God's purpose and God's plan as revealed in the Bible so that we will know how to pray.

The good news about prayer is that the prayers of a righteous person can change a life, a home, a marriage, a church, a school, a community, an entire nation. "The effective, fervent prayer of a righteous man avails much" (James 5:16).

Daniel took prayer seriously. He "prayed with fasting, sackcloth, and ashes" (Daniel 9:3). Daniel was so focused on prayer that he did not eat. "Sackcloth and ashes" was a manner of praying that demonstrated humility and sorrow for sin. If we want to pray like Daniel, we need to have the same serious attitude about prayer. He humbled himself before the Lord and was truly repentant and concerned for the people of God.

WHAT CAN WE LEARN FROM DANIEL AS HE BEGAN TO PRAY?

1) Confession is an essential ingredient in our prayers. Repentance is necessary and must be a regular part of our prayer time.

2) Focus on the Lord. Our focus must not be on the problem, or friends who might help, or even our need. Our focus must be on the Lord. We must keep our eyes on Jesus.

3) We must take prayer seriously. We may tend to ignore prayer, or regard it glibly, except in a crisis. Prayer should be from our heart of devotion and love for the Lord. It should be a part of the fabric of our lives.

4) Prayer, like our faith, must be experienced. Books about prayer have their place, but prayer is not so much taught as it is caught. Just do it!

5) Difficult, chaotic times. When Daniel saw difficult times coming, he prayed. We are living in chaotic times, and as believers, we should be immersed in prayer. Only the Lord knows the future. Only the Lord can guide your journey safely home to heaven.

The questions are: Are you serious about prayer, and have you set your face toward the Lord? When Daniel faced a chaotic future, he looked to the Lord. We must do the same.

CHAPTER 13

Daniel's Prayer
For His People
Daniel 9:4-19

In the ninth chapter of the Book of Daniel is recorded the powerful prayer that Daniel prayed for his people. The question may come to your mind, does prayer make a difference with God? The answer is yes! Prayer makes a difference to God when it makes a difference to you. Do your prayers originate in a deep devotion and faith in the Lord? Are you consistent in your prayer times and in your obedience to the Lord? If you want your prayers to change things, let them first change you. Your prayer life could change your habits, your priorities, your schedule, your values, and your focus. When that happens, your prayers will be more like Daniel's prayers.

In this prayer Daniel described the sin of the nation in light of God's character. He agreed with God's righteous judgment and then asked God to restore His people to their land.

Powerful Prayer is Personal

Nine times in his prayer, Daniel included himself by using the personal pronoun "we." Seventeen times Daniel said, "us" and "our." He was not vague. He included himself. Daniel prayed: "… we have sinned and committed iniquity, we have done wickedly and rebelled, even by departing from Your precepts and Your judgements" (Daniel 9:5). This is a prayer of repentance for their past sinfulness.

Daniel used several different words to describe Israel's sin: "sin" means "to miss the mark"; "miss the target"; "iniquity" means "twisted." They had "twisted" or "perverted" God's truth. "Wickedly" means "deliberate evil." Their sin was no accident. "Rebelled" means they intentionally decided to go against God's precepts.

POWERFUL PRAYER IS BASED ON GOD'S CHARACTER

1) Daniel prayed: "O Lord, great and awesome God, who keeps His covenant and mercy with those who love Him, and with those who keep His commandments ..." (Daniel 9:4). In the first part of verse 4, Daniel said he "prayed to the Lord my God." "Lord" in Hebrew is the consonants YHWH, which is the personal name that God revealed to Moses in the burning bush. Daniel prayed to Yahweh, the Creator who delivered the children of Israel from 400 years of bondage in Egypt.

Today it is common to call many things or people "great" or "awesome." But only the Lord God Almighty is great, and He only inspires awe and wonder and respect at the highest level. God "keeps or guards" His covenant. The Lord keeps His Word. He alone is faithful. Not only does the Lord keep His covenant Word, He showers grace and mercy on those who love Him.

2) "Righteousness belongs to You" (Daniel 9:7). The Lord alone is always right. The Bible declares about us: "Our righteousness is as filthy rags" (Isaiah 64:6). We are made to be righteous, right with God, through the blood of Jesus Christ shed on the cross.

3) "Mercy and forgiveness" belong to the Lord (Daniel 9:9). The Lord is the author of one salvation. He is the only One who is able to forgive our sins.

4) *Our Deliverer.* "And now, O Lord our God, who brought Your people out of the land of Egypt with a mighty hand, and made yourself a name ..." (Daniel 9:15). Because the Lord delivered the Israelites from Egypt, led them safely through the Red Sea, and brought them to the promised land, His name was well known among the nations. One day all will bow before Jesus whose name is above every name: "Therefore God also has highly exalted Him and given Him the name which is above every name, that at the name of Jesus every knee should bow, of those in heaven, and of those on earth, and of those under the earth, and that every tongue should confess that Jesus Christ is Lord, to the glory of God the Father" (Philippians 2:9-11).

POWERFUL PRAYER IS WITHOUT EXCUSE

When we sin we may often say: "I goofed," or "I blew it," or "I made a mistake," or "that was bad judgment," or "my bad," or "well, everybody makes mistakes." Or, we tend to blame others for leading us astray or confusing us in some way. Daniel did not blame Israel's enemies for their moral failure. He did not blame the Canaanites, the Philistines, the Syrians or the Babylonians. The Israelites had missed the mark, perverted God's ways, trespassed God's law and rebelled against God's leadership over them.

We must admit our sin. We should take responsibility for our actions; we must own our moral failure. Instead of justifying ourselves and blaming others, we need to confess our sin and seek the Lord's forgiveness.

Daniel confessed their sins, and he knew they deserved the judgment that had come to them. Three times Daniel used the word "disaster" (Daniel 9:12, 13, 14) when referring to their captivity. Daniel knew that Israel had been challenged to repent, but they had refused, and the Lord's judgment came. But in His mercy, the Lord had set a limit to their captivity. We must accept responsibility for our actions.

POWERFUL PRAYER INCLUDES PETITION

Daniel began his prayer "with fasting, sackcloth, and ashes" (Daniel 9:3). He was in the proper position and attitude of humility before the Lord. Next, Daniel praised the "great and awesome God" (Daniel 9:4). Then Daniel confessed his sin and the sin of the people before God: "We have not obeyed the voice of the Lord our God ..." (Daniel 9:10). Daniel, on behalf of the people, took responsibility for their sin: "... (W)e have rebelled against Him" (Daniel 9:9). After all of this, Daniel made his requests of the Lord.

Beginning in verse 16 Daniel made this request of the Lord: "(L)et Your anger and Your fury be turned away from Your city Jerusalem and Your holy mountain" (Daniel 9:16). "Now therefore, our God, hear the prayer of Your servant, ... for the Lord's sake cause Your face to shine on Your sanctuary which is desolate" (Daniel 9:17). "O my God, incline Your ear and hear; open Your eyes and see our desolations ... we do not present our supplications before You because of our righteous deeds, but because of your great mercies" (Daniel 9:18). In verse 19, Daniel cried out, "hear, forgive, listen, act, do not delay." These requests were not made on the basis of their merit; they had not earned nor deserved God's forgiveness. Daniel's plea was based on the mercy of God. Paul wrote: "Be anxious for nothing, but in everything by prayer and supplication, with thanksgiving, let your requests be made known to God; and the peace of God, which surpasses all understanding, will guard your hearts and minds through Christ Jesus" (Philippians 4:6-7).

WHAT DO WE LEARN FROM DANIEL'S PRAYER?

1) Prayer springs from the Word of God. As we read and study the Bible, we discover our sin and that should break our hearts and drive us to our knees in repentance. Daniel was reading Jeremiah and realized what God was doing, and so Daniel began to pray.

2) Prayer is focused on the will of God. Daniel discovered that it was the will of the Lord for Israel to be in the Babylonian captivity for seventy years. Daniel prayed that he and the people would be ready to serve the Lord when their captivity was over.

In the Garden of Gethsemane Jesus prayed: "O My Father, if it is possible, let this cup pass from Me; nevertheless, not as I will, but as You will" (Matthew 26:39). Jesus did not want to be separated from His Father and become sin for us, but more than that, Jesus wanted to do His Father's will.

I'm sure this is not an original thought, but it struck me while studying Daniel. It is that prayer is essentially agreeing with Jesus. Prayer includes different aspects like adoration, confession, thanksgiving and petition. But it must all be in agreement with the will and purpose of Jesus. We must pray, "not my will, but thine be done."

3) Prayer must be serious. Daniel "set his face toward the Lord God to make requests by prayer and supplications, with fasting, sackcloth, and ashes" (Daniel 9:3). Daniel was passionate about prayer. A church that is alive is a praying church.

4) Spiritual warfare. Satan is a deceiver and always is seeking to destroy people's lives. "Be sober, be vigilant; because your adversary the devil walks about like a roaring lion, seeking whom he may devour" (1 Peter 5:8). Prayer is our weapon in this warfare. Satan attacks Christians, their families, the church and other organizations that are following Christ. This is war! We must pray. When Daniel realized the situation, he prayed.

The challenge for all of us today is to make a serious commitment to regular, fervent prayer. Several years ago, I challenged our church to begin a personal prayer time. I challenged them to commit to "Fifteen Minutes with The Master" as a starting point. Think about your prayer times. How much time do you spend in prayer? Are you really serious about prayer?

CHAPTER 14

THE TOUCH OF GOD
DANIEL 9:20-24

I like the words of a Gaither song, "He Touched Me." In His earthly ministry Jesus is pictured constantly reaching out, touching, and healing others. The lame, the blind, the lepers, Jesus healed all who came to Him. "When evening had come, they brought to Him many who were demon-possessed. And He cast out the spirits with a word, and healed all who were sick ..." (Matthew 8:16). Daniel had been praying and the Lord God answered. The first result of the prayer was that he was touched by Gabriel.

HE TOUCHED ME

Daniel said that while he was "praying and confessing my sin and the sin of my people Israel ... before the Lord God ... the man Gabriel ... reached me about the time of the evening offering" (Daniel 9:20-21). The word "reach" in Hebrew literally means "touch." While Daniel was praying, the Lord, through the angel Gabriel, touched him. What we need most as an answer to pray is the Lord's touch on our lives! The more we pray, the more we are aware of the Lord's presence. If you want to feel the hand of the Lord in your life, then pray.

When we pray, we don't demand things from the Lord, the Lord commands us. The Lord has a plan for your life, just as He had a plan for Daniel's life. In prayer we begin to understand the will of the Lord for our lives.

THREE O'CLOCK

While Daniel was praying, the angel "reached" or "touched" him: "about the time of the evening offering" (Daniel 9:21). When the Jews had a temple in Jerusalem, the priests burned incense at 3 p.m. Incense symbolized that the prayers of the people were going up to the Lord. It was also the time for the evening offering. A lamb would be offered for the sin of the people. There was no temple, but Daniel was praying at the hour of the evening offering.

Remember, Jesus was on the cross at this time of day. "Now from the sixth hour (noon) until the ninth hour (3 p.m.) there was darkness over all the land" (Matthew 27:45). Matthew also wrote that at the ninth hour "Jesus cried out again with a loud voice, and yielded up His spirit" (Matthew 27: 46, 50). Every time I think of that, chills run up and down my spine. The Lord God had all this planned out ,and these events all happened at 3 p.m. Three o'clock in the afternoon is a great time to pray; of course, anytime is a great time to pray.

AT THE BEGINNING

Gabriel told Daniel that he had come to give Daniel understanding (Daniel 9:22). The surprising thing is that Gabriel told Daniel that the Lord sent him as an answer to Daniel's prayer: "At the beginning of your supplications ..." (Daniel 9:23). This was a quick reply directly from the Lord and hand delivered by Gabriel. Daniel had been praying and confessing his and his people's sin and asking God for forgiveness. But Daniel received so much more.

1) Gabriel told Daniel, "You are greatly loved" (Daniel 9:23). If you are a believer, do you remember when you first realized that you were loved by the Lord? What a glorious thing it is to know that the Lord loves us so much that He sent His Son Jesus to die on a cross to pay the penalty for our sin.

2) Daniel was loved so much that the Lord issued the command for Gabriel to go to Daniel when he began to pray. The Lord knows our thoughts and our actions. He wants to see us humbled before Him, confessing our adoration and our sin and our need for Him. "For your Father knows the things you have need of before you ask Him" (Matthew 6:8). Spend time in prayer listening to what the Lord wants to reveal to you.

THE MESSAGE

1) Seventy weeks. This may also be translated "seventy-sevens" (Daniel 9:24). A seventy "week" exile would last for seven times seventy years. This would mean that it would be 490 years before God's people would have complete reconciliation with God. This would be the time lapse before the coming of the Messiah. Since seven is the number of completion, it means when the Lord has all things completed in His plan the Messiah will come. In verse 25, Gabriel stated: "(T)hat from the going forth of the command to restore and build Jerusalem until Messiah the Prince, there shall be seven weeks and sixty-two weeks ... ."

In Nehemiah 2, the decree of Artaxerxes was given to Nehemiah to return to Jerusalem to rebuild the wall of the city. The seven weeks and sixty-two weeks of verse 20 would result in 483 years. The decree of Artaxerxes was in 445 BC. The end of the sixty-nine weeks is the date of the crucifixion of Jesus! Jesus is "Messiah the Prince." Artaxerxes began ruling in 465 BC. In his twentieth year he signed the decree, which would be 445 BC. Add in the sixty-two sevens and the year would be AD 32.

2) The Messiah's sacrificial death. "Messiah shall be cut off, but not for Himself" (Daniel 9:26). Jesus was executed like a common criminal on a cross. The verb "cut off" means "executed as a criminal." Jesus hung on the cross between two thieves. Jesus' death was "not for Himself." Jesus died on the cross to pay the penalty for our sins.

Daniel, and the Jews, did not know that the Messiah, Jesus, would come twice. After Jesus' death on the cross and His resurrection, He ascended to heaven. But He is coming again. "I go to prepare a place for you. And if I go and prepare a place for you, I will come again and receive you to Myself; that where I am, there you may be also" (John 14:2-3).

Gabriel told Daniel that the Messiah would "finish the transgression" (Daniel 9:24). "Transgression" means "trespass." The people had crossed over or trespassed God's forbidden boundary and were living outside of the law delivered to Moses. Transgression would be "finished" by the Messiah. The Messiah will "make an end of sins" (Daniel 9:24). "Sin" means "to miss the mark." The Lord had a plan for His people, but they deliberately missed the target; they missed God's good for their lives. That too will come to an end. The Messiah will "make reconciliation for iniquity," which means that the Messiah "will atone for perversion" (Daniel 9:24). The people's minds were "twisted," warped by sin. They had taken what was decent and distorted it.

These three definitions of evil doing were atoned for by Jesus on the cross. Yet all three will be finally destroyed when Jesus comes again and the final judgment occurs. The revelation to Daniel was about the saving work of Jesus when He came the first time, and also about the final victory of the King of kings and Lord of lords when Jesus comes again.

3) The Messiah's victory. Not only will the Messiah conquer all sin, He will "bring in everlasting righteousness." We can only be right with

God and right with others by the transforming power of Jesus Christ. That righteousness will be "everlasting" when all believers are gathered before the throne of God. "And every creature which is in heaven and on the earth and under the earth and such as are in the sea, and all that are in them, I heard saying: "Blessing and honor and glory and power be to Him who sits on the throne, and to the Lamb, forever and ever!" (Revelation 5:13).

"Vision and prophecy" will be "sealed up" (Daniel 9:24). When Jesus comes again, there will be no need for vision or prophecy, because we will see Jesus face to face. We will "know as we are known." The Lord will bring all of history to completion.

The Messiah will "anoint the Most Holy" (Daniel 9:24). Jesus will consecrate the Holy Place in the temple in the future that will be a part of the millennial kingdom. Ezekiel described the new temple in a vision from the Lord and is recorded in Ezekiel 40-48.

'WHEN WILL THESE THINGS BE?'

1) The disciples asked Jesus that question (Matthew 24:3). After Jesus had discussed some signs of the end times, He responded: "But of that day and hour no one knows, not even the angels of heaven, but My Father only. ... Therefore you also be ready, for the Son of Man is coming at an hour you do not expect" (Matthew 24:36, 44).

"And the people of the prince who is to come shall destroy the city and the sanctuary ..." (Daniel 9:26). This destructive prince must be the Antichrist. Daniel earlier called him the "little horn." The "people" who belonged to the Antichrist destroyed the temple in AD 70. The Roman army under the leadership of Titus destroyed Jerusalem and the temple just as Jesus had predicted: "... not one stone shall be left here upon another that shall not be thrown down" (Matthew 24:2). "And till the end of the war desolations are determined" (Daniel 9:26), and Jesus said, "And you will hear of wars and rumors of wars" (Matthew 24:6).

2) *Last week.* The Lord had been preparing everything for what was announced in verse 27. The Antichrist will make a covenant with Israel for one week of years or seven years (Daniel 9:27). But in the middle of that time the Antichrist will stop sacrifice and offering and break the covenant. "Abominations" and "desolate" describe the blasphemy of the Antichrist against the Lord. "Even until the consummation" means that this abomination occurs at the end time. This is not the abomination of Antiochus or any other evil person, but of the Antichrist. The Antichrist will call for everyone to worship him. "So they worshiped the dragon who gave authority to the beast; and they worshiped the beast ..." (Revelation 13:4). This period lasts for forty-two months: "And they will tread the holy city underfoot for forty-two months" (Revelation 11:2). Forty-two months, or three and a half years, will be this period of abomination. "(T)he man of sin is revealed, the son of perdition, who opposes and exalts himself above all that is called God or that is worshiped, so that he sits as God in the temple of God, showing himself that he is God" (2 Thessalonians 2:4). Many leaders in history have called themselves gods, and the Antichrist is the final one. The Antichrist will not allow anyone to be worshiped but himself.

Although many men have wanted to have absolute power and rule like God, the true God became a man, and redeemed all who come to Him in faith by the shedding of His blood on the cross (Philippians 2:6-8). The Lord deserves all worship and praise. He does not demand it, but invites us to come to Him freely.

WHAT ARE THE MAIN LESSONS FROM THESE VERSES?

1) *It is the deep desire of the Lord to touch your life.* The Lord touched Daniel and told him he was greatly loved. The Lord has written you a long love letter — the Bible! The Lord loves you and wants to touch your

life with His saving power.

2) *Accuracy of the Word of God.* These verses revealed the exact time of the return of the Jews to their homeland from their captivity in Babylon. These verses also revealed the exact time of the coming of the Messiah, the Lord Jesus, the first time.

3) *We are not forsaken.* The Lord will not forsake His followers. The Jews were sad when they were taken into captivity. Through the prophet Daniel, the Lord showed He was present with them and that He had a plan to take them home.

America is saddened by our hasty withdrawal from Afghanistan that left many Americans and our allies behind enemy lines. But our Lord will not leave His followers behind. Jesus is coming back to take us home to be with Him. "Blessed are the dead who die in the Lord from now on. Yes, says the Spirit, that they may rest from their labors, and their works follow them" (Revelation 14:13).

4) *The kingdom of Jesus is coming.* Jesus will "finish transgression," "make an end of sin," and "make reconciliation for iniquity," and "bring in everlasting righteousness" (Daniel 9:24). Our victorious Christ is coming in power and judgment and to gather the faithful unto Himself.

In the midst of your dark times, the Lord Jesus will come to you, and reveal that He loves you, and offers you forgiveness and hope. Jesus stands with open arms to all who call upon His name.

CHAPTER 15

JESUS CAME DOWN
DANIEL 10:1-21

In the tenth chapter of Daniel, he received his fourth revelation. The vision and the explanation of the vision will continue to the end of the Book of Daniel.

TIME AND PLACE OF THE VISION

It was the "third year of Cyrus king of Persia," which would have been 536 BC (Daniel 10:1). Daniel "was mourning" because he wanted to understand the vision. This is seen by what was written in verse 12: "Do not fear, Daniel, for from the first day that you set your heart to understand, and to humble yourself before your God, your words were heard, and I have come because of your words" (Daniel 10:12).

From this verse we realize Daniel had been praying. In the midst of every crisis Daniel prayed. This ought to teach us something. When was the last time your heart was broken over the condition of your family, your friends, your church, or your country? Has your heart been broken by the evil you see in our society today? If so, you will pray.

Daniel had been "mourning three full weeks" (Daniel 10:2). Daniel was observing the Passover and the Feast of Unleavened Bread, which occurred the first month of the Jewish year (cf. Exodus 12:1-20). The

Passover was observed on the fourteenth of the month, and the Feast of Unleavened Bread for the next eight days. The whole observance was over on the twenty-first of the month. Verse three described the observance. The Passover was the most important of the holy observances on the Jewish calendar. Passover commemorated the death angel "passing over" the Jewish homes in Egypt whose families had obeyed God. They sacrificed a lamb, sprinkled the blood around their door, cooked and ate the lamb meat, with bitter herbs and bread baked in haste. So it was unleavened, because there was no time for the bread to rise with leaven and be baked.

"(O)n the twenty-fourth day of the first month, as I was by the side of the great river that is the Tigris ..." (Daniel 10:4). Now three days after the end of the festival of Unleavened Bread, Daniel was by the Tigris River, or "Hiddekel" in Hebrew.

So it was on the twenty-fourth day of the first month in 536 BC, three days after the festival of Unleavened Bread, that Daniel was by the Tigris River, apparently in prayer. Perhaps Daniel was discouraged, because when the opportunity came for the Jews to return to Jerusalem, only a little more than 42,000 went back, according to Ezra. Some of the Jews had become paganized, or were comfortable and prosperous, and would not go back. Going back to Jerusalem was difficult and dangerous. It took months to clear the rubble on the temple mount; there was the wall to rebuild, and crops to plant and harvest; and they were opposed by those who dwelt near Jerusalem.

THE VISION

1) "A certain man." This was an appearance of the preincarnate Christ, as we can see from the description in verse 6. John's description of Jesus found in Revelation Chapter 1 is similar: "One like the Son of Man, clothed with a garment down to the feet and girded about the chest with a golden band. His head and hair were white like wool, as white as snow, and His eyes like flame of fire; His feet were like fine brass ... . His voice as the sound of many waters ... . His countenance was like the sun shining in its strength (Revelation 1:13-16).

2) Daniel's description of the exalted Christ. He was "clothed in linen." The linen would represent God's holiness, the purity of God. The description in Revelation of "white hair" could also represent Jesus' holiness. His "waist girded with the gold of Uphaz" in Daniel compares to the description in Revelation of Jesus "girded with a golden band." "His body was like beryl" (Daniel 10:6) compares to "clothed with a garment down to His feet" in Revelation. The long garment meant that the glorified Christ described in Revelation is dressed like a high priest. This compares to Daniel's vision of "His body was like beryl." Beryl is a transparent and very flashy jewel. It stood for the glory of God revealed in Jesus. The white appearance is similar to the description of the Ancient of Days in Daniel 7:9 and of Christ on the Mount of Transfiguration (Matthew 17:2). Believers who overcome will be "clothed in white garments" (Revelation 3:5), which symbolizes purity.

His "face like lightning" in Daniel is similar to His "countenance was like the sun shining" in Revelation. This described the power and presence of the glory of the Lord. His "eyes like torches of fire" compares to "eyes like a flame of fire" in Revelation. Jesus' penetrating eyesight sees all, even our hearts and minds.

"Feet like burnished bronze" and "feet like fine brass" speak of power. The description of the "sound of His words like the voice of a multitude" (Daniel 10:6) is similar to "and His voice as the sound of many waters" (Revelation 1:15). This means that His voice is powerful and will be heard by everyone.

The comparison would be like this:

Daniel	Revelation
"clothed in linen"	"clothed with a garment down to His feet"
"waist girded with gold"	"girded with a golden band"
"His body was the beryl"	"white hair" and the long garment
"face like lightning"	"countenance was like the sun shining"
"eyes like torches of fire"	"eyes like a flame of fire"
"arms and feet like burnished bronze"	"feet like fine brass"
"sound of His words like the voice of a multitude"	"voice like the sound of many waters"

These descriptions make it clear that this is an Old Testament appearance of the Lord Jesus Christ to Daniel in this vision. In the Old Testament, the phrase "the angel of the Lord" occurs at least fifty times. Often the Bible then states, "and God said" (see Genesis 16:9-13 and Joshua 6:11-14, for example). In the Old Testament Jesus came as protector, advocate, to comfort Hagar, and to commission men like Moses, Gideon, Samson and others to follow Him. In Daniel Chapter 3, there were three placed in the fiery furnace, but when Nebuchadnezzar looked he saw a fourth "like unto the Son of God." In Daniel Chapter 7, Daniel had a vision of the throne of God and one came "like unto the Son of Man." Jesus was involved with His Father in creation (John 1:3) and has been working all through history.

DANIEL'S REACTION

1) Daniel saw the vision, but those with him did not see it, but they were terrified, and they left (Daniel 10:7). Daniel's "strength" and "vigor" left him, and he was weak and frail in the presence of the Lord (Daniel 10:8). Although he could hear the words, Daniel was face down on the ground (Daniel 10:9). The angel of the Lord "touched" Daniel, and he began to "tremble" (Daniel 10:10). Daniel was so frightened that his hands and knees were shaking. When John had his vision of the Lord, he wrote: "And when I saw Him, I fell at His feet as dead" (Revelation 1:17).

The angel spoke to Daniel, reassuring him that he was "greatly beloved," and told Daniel to "stand upright" and the angel would explain. In Revelation, Jesus placed His hand on John and said: "Do not be afraid" (Revelation 1:17).

2) The delay. In verses 12 and 13, the angel explained his delay in coming to Daniel. From the start of Daniel's prayer to understand and humble himself before God, he was heard by the Lord (Daniel 10:12). "But the prince of Persia withstood me twenty-one days ..." (Daniel 10:13). The conflict was a spiritual conflict. This prince was a satanic figure over Persia to inspire the people there to do evil. Paul referred to "principalities, powers, rulers of darkness," and "spiritual hosts of wickedness in the heavenly places" (Ephesians 6:12). The angel was detained for "twenty-one days," which is the time of Daniel's mourning and fasting (Daniel 10:2-3). The wicked prince of Persia tried to keep Daniel from hearing more of God's revelation (Daniel 10:14). "Michael, one of the chief princes, came to help me ..." (Daniel 10:13). Michael seems to be one of the most powerful angels. Michael is mentioned three times in Daniel (Daniel 10:13, 21; 12:1) and two times in the New Testament (Jude 9, Revelation 12:7).

The angel revealed the reality that we are involved In spiritual warfare on earth and in the heavens. Apparently, Satan has organized his demons and assigned them to the nations. He mentioned the "prince of Persia" and the "prince of Greece" (Daniel 10:20). The work of Satan and his demons is to interrupt the will and the work of the Lord in His people wherever Christians serve. What are we to do? Pray! Pray against Satan. "Resist the devil and he will flee from you" (James 4:7).

Paul wrote that because of the work of Christ on the cross (Colossians 2:15) that "(h)aving disarmed principalities and powers, He made a public spectacle of them, triumphing over them ..." (Colossians 2:15).

3) The time of the vision. The vision concerned "what will happen to your people in the latter days, for the vision refers to many days yet to come" (Daniel 10:14). The messenger is referring to what will be revealed in Daniel Chapter 11.

4) Daniel was overwhelmed and looked down and "became speechless" (Daniel 10:15). Then "one having the likeness of the son of man touched my lips" (Daniel 10:16). "One" and "son of man" probably means this is an appearance of Jesus to Daniel. This time He touched Daniel's lips so he could speak. Daniel said, "My Lord, because of the vision my sorrows have overwhelmed me, and I have retained no strength" (Daniel 10:16). Because of his lack of strength, he could speak no more (Daniel 10:17). "One having the likeness of a man ..." strengthened Daniel. And for the third time wrote that he "touched me" (Daniel 10:18). Again, Daniel was reassured. Daniel was addressed as "greatly beloved"; was told to "fear not"; a "peace" blessing was given to him; and he was challenged to "be strong!" (Daniel 10:19). This sounds so much like the New Testament words of Jesus. When Jesus approached His disciples walking on the water, Jesus said, "Fear not" (Matthew 14:27). Jesus encouraged His disciples before he went to the cross: "Peace I leave with you, My peace I give to you. Let not your heart be troubled, neither let it be afraid" (John 14:27). The gift of Jesus' perfect peace is the cure for our fears.

For the third time in this chapter, Daniel was "strengthened" by one who "touched" him (Daniel 10:10, 16, 18). The messenger of God told Daniel he would have to resume his spiritual battle with the "prince of Persia" and the "prince of Greece," but he would have the help of Michael (Daniel 10:20-21).

In order for us to fight our spiritual battles, we need to be strengthened by the touch of the Lord Jesus in our lives. Can you testify, "He touched me and changed my life"?

WHAT INSIGHTS DO WE DISCOVER IN THESE VERSES?

1) These verses give us insight into the holiness, glory, and majesty of the preincarnate Christ as He revealed Himself to Daniel.

2) These verses give us insight into the role of Jesus in the Old Testament. Jesus was present, involved, and working with His Father in the lives of people in Old Testament times.

3) These verses give us insight into the spiritual warfare that was then and continues to this day between God's angels and the demons. We are affected by that warfare, and we can be effective in spiritual warfare as we pray and put on the whole armor of God (Ephesians 6:11).

4) These verses give us insight into the heart of Daniel. Daniel was a man of prayer and he gained his strength and wisdom through the touch of the Lord in his life.

5) These verses give us insight into the truth that the secret of powerful intercessory prayer is a broken heart. Daniel's heart was broken over his sin and the sin of his people.

6) These verses give us insight into the grace of the Lord, because He touches weak people and they speak for Him. The Lord can touch your life and your life can be lived for Him.

It is my prayer that Jesus will touch your heart today. Jesus' touch can save you, strengthen you, and enable you to be used by Him to do anything He wants you to accomplish.

CHAPTER 16

THE 'A' LIST OF
THE WORLD'S EVIL LEADERS
DANIEL 11:1-39

In our short 245-year history, the United States has fought many wars. Almost all of these battles were fought on foreign soil. One of our most deadly wars was our Civil War. There were more battles fought in Tennessee than any other state except for Virginia. One of the reasons is that Tennessee was a border state and was caught in the middle of that great conflict.

Israel is in that same kind of situation. Mankind has been in rebellion against God ever since the Garden of Eden. Wars have swirled all around and in Israel from Bible times until today. People have defied God and sought to destroy His followers. This will continue until Jesus comes again.

In Chapter 11 of Daniel, he was given a glimpse into the future. Israel would be caught in the middle as powerful armies from Syria and Egypt fought each other. One way to understand this difficult chapter is to focus on the leaders of the nations involved.

AHASUERUS OR XERXES

1) *"The first year of Darius"* (Daniel 11:1). This is the same year

as the revelation of seventy weeks, 539 BC (Daniel 9:1). At the start of the Persian rule in Babylon, the messenger from the Lord "stood up to confirm and strengthen him" (Daniel 11:1). The Lord had a purpose even for the pagan ruler Darius. The kingdoms of this world are under demonic control, but human leaders can be delivered from that control and be used by the Lord for His purpose.

2) *"Three more kings ... and the fourth"* (Daniel 11:2). Darius, who ruled under Cyrus, was followed by Cambyses (520-522 BC); Gammata (522 BC); Darius I (522-486 BC); and Xerxes (486-465 BC). The fourth was "far richer" due to his conquest and severe taxation of his people. Xerxes tried to conquer Greece (Daniel 11:2). During his reign Xerxes was defeated by the Greeks. His kingdom extended from India to Ethiopia. He ruled from his royal residence in Shushan, which was the location of one of Daniel's visions (Daniel 8:2). He is the ruler in the Book of Esther, and Xerxes executed Haman for his evil plot (Esther 1:3, 7:9).

ALEXANDER THE GREAT

1) *"A mighty king shall arise ..."* (Daniel 11:3). This king was Alexander the Great who went on to conquer the entire region. By age thirty-three Alexander had conquered a region extending from Europe to India. When Alexander died, his kingdom was fought over and finally four of his generals divided the kingdom (Daniel 11:4; 8:22). "But not his posterity" means that his heirs received nothing (Daniel 11:4).

2) *The two parts of Alexander's former empire* that affected Israel were the Seleucids, who ruled in Syria to the North, and the Ptolemais, who ruled in Egypt to the South. So every time they fought each other they would plunder Israel. These two are the "North " and "South" references in Daniel Chapter 11 (Daniel 11:5-9, 11, 13-15, 25, 40).

3) *Often alliances between nations were secured by marriage.*

So the king in the North put away his wife and married an Egyptian (Daniel 11:6). The daughter refers to Berenice, the daughter of Ptolemy (285-246 BC) of Egypt. "The king of the North" refers to Antiochus II Theos (261-246 BC) of Syria. This alliance was a failure (Daniel 11:6b).

ANTIOCHUS III THE GREAT

1) "But from a branch of her roots one shall arise ..." (Daniel 11:7). One of Berenice's brothers took control of Egypt and marched on the king of the North and prevailed (Daniel 11:7). He plundered Syria and returned to Egypt. There is continued warfare between the two, and their marauding armies would pass through Israel causing strife (Daniel 11:9-10). The "king of the South," Ptolemy IV (221-204 BC) defeated "the king of the North," Antiochus III the Great in 217 BC (Daniel 11:11). The "king of the North" assembled a great army and attacked Egypt in 201 BC.

2) "Many shall rise up ..." (Daniel 11:14) meant that others like Philip V of Macedon helped Antiochus fight against Ptolemy V (203-181 BC) of Egypt. "Violent men of your people ... in fulfillment of the vision, but they shall fail" (Daniel 11:14b). There were Jews who tried to help Antiochus bring to pass what had been predicted in the vision of Chapter 8 of Daniel, but they failed. "The king of the North," Antiochus, defeated the "fortified city" of Sidon in 198 BC. "The Glorious Land" referred to Israel. The control of Palestine passed from Egypt to Syria.

In 201 BC, Antiochus II of Syria defeated the Ptolemais of Egypt with the help of the Jews. The Jews were free from the Egyptians until 175 BC. Antiochus IV oppressed the Jews which led to the Maccabean Revolt of 167 BC and Jewish freedom in 164 BC.

3) Cleopatra. Antiochus III's daughter Cleopatra was given in marriage to Ptolemy V of Egypt in order to undermine Egypt, but Cleopatra sided with her husband and not her father (Daniel 4:17).

4) Rome. As their battles continued, Egypt asked for help from a new power, Rome. The Romans sent their fleet to Egypt, and the Syrians fled. The Romans defeated Antiochus, and he returned to "his own land," where he was defeated and killed while trying to plunder a temple (Daniel 11:1-19).

5) Seleucis IV (187-176 BC). "Arise in his place" referred to Antiochus' son, who took his father's place (Daniel 11:20). He taxed the "glorious kingdom," which referred to Israel. He raised taxes to pay tribute to Rome.

ANTIOCHUS EPIPHANES

1) "A vile person" referred to Antiochus IV Epiphanes (175-164 BC), who gained the throne through treachery (Daniel 11:21). They shall be "swept away" referred to the swiftness of his defeat of his enemies. "The prince of the covenant" referred to the high priest in Jerusalem who was overcome by Antiochus (Daniel 11:22). Antiochus used deceit, entered peacefully and took control. He dispersed the spoils among his followers (Daniel 11:23-24).

2) War with Egypt. Antiochus attacked the "king of the South" (Ptolemy 181-145 BC) of Egypt. But Ptolemy's own counselors who ate at his table betrayed him, and he was defeated (Daniel 11:25-26). "Both these kings' hearts shall be bent on evil" (Daniel 11:27). Both Antiochus and Ptolemy were deceitful in working out truce arrangements.

3) "The holy covenant" referred to Israel. On his way back to Syria, Antiochus looted the temple in Jerusalem and killed many of the Jews (Daniel 11:28). Again, Antiochus marched south to war with Egypt, but ships from Cyprus came against him, and in rage he turned against the "holy covenant" and "did damage" (Daniel 11:29-30). "Those who forsake the holy covenant" were those Jews who abandoned faith in God and sided with Antiochus (Daniel 11:30). "Defile the sanctuary" referred to Antiochus polluting the altar by offering a pig on it. He ruled that all the "daily sacrifices" were illegal and erected an idol of Zeus in the holy place, which was the "abomination of desolation" (Daniel 11:31). Antiochus "corrupted with flattery" those who did "wickedly against the covenant," but the faithful "who know their God shall be strong, and carry out great exploits" (Daniel 11:32). Matthias and his sons refused to offer pagan sacrifices and rebelled against Antiochus. They fled to the mountains and organized a revolt. Many Jews were killed in this revolt (Daniel 11:33-34); the faithful were allowed to go through this difficult time "to refine them, to purify them" (Daniel 11:35).

THE ANTICHRIST

In the closing words of verse 35, it states: "until the time of the end; because it is still for the appointed time." Most interpreters believe that the following verses describe the Antichrist. "He shall magnify himself above every god, shall speak blasphemies against the God of gods ..." perfectly describes the work of the Antichrist (Daniel 11:36).

"He shall not regard the God of his fathers," the God his ancestors worshiped, "nor the desire of women," the worship of female goddesses (Daniel 11:37). The Antichrist will only worship the "god of fortresses," meaning the god of power (Daniel 11:38). He will go to war with others and rule over them (Daniel 11:39).

In verses 40-45 is a summary of the battles of the Antichrist and his covenant with Israel. He is attacked by the kings of the North and the South, but he overwhelms them (Daniel 11:401). He enters "the Glorious Land" but spares Edom, Moab, and Ammon, enemies of Israel (Daniel 11:41). He will then conquer Egypt, Libya, and Ethiopia (Daniel 11:42-43). His battles continue in verse 44. He rules ("his place") between the seas (the Mediterranean Sea and the Dead Sea) and "the glorious holy mountain." The holy mountain is Mount Zion in Jerusalem, the site of the temple. The end for the Antichrist will come and "no one will help him" (Daniel 11:45). The end for the Antichrist will be when our Lord Jesus Christ comes in final judgment (Revelation 19:11-21).

WHAT DOES ALL OF THIS MEAN FOR US TODAY?

1) It is a reminder that the Lord God is in control of history. The Lord revealed 200 years of the future to Daniel. The Lord also revealed events of the last days.

2) It is a reminder that we are living in the end times. Who would have thought we would be living in a day in which we would need to define what is a man or a woman? We are living in a world of abomination. Many have forsaken the Lord and turned to gods of power or money. But those "who know their God shall be strong" (Daniel 11:32). We must stand for the truth of the Lord Jesus Christ and live a life that is pleasing to Him and not be led astray by the world.

3) It is a reminder that one purpose of suffering is to refine us and purify us (Daniel 11:35). Suffering can open our eyes to the presence of Christ.

4) It is a reminder that there is only one eternal covenant. There was much intrigue, plotting, false agreements, and wars described in Daniel Chapter 11. Multiply that by all of human history since that time. There is one covenant that has been written that will stand forever. It was a covenant written with the blood of the Lord Jesus Christ. That covenant will stand, not because we are strong or brave, but because the Lord Jesus Christ will keep His word.

5) It is a reminder that Israel is the battleground. That was true in the past and is true today. Many Hamas rockets were fired into Israel this year. The last great battle will be found at Armageddon, which means the "valley of Megiddo in" Israel. There the forces of evil will be arrayed against the Lord, but they will be destroyed by the word of the Lord.

The hope of this world is Jesus Christ. We are living in a world of darkness, but Jesus is the light. He is our hope. He is shining in our darkness now, and He is ready to give us peace. If you sense the darkness around you, turn to Jesus and He will light your way home to Him.

CHAPTER 17

HOPE IN TRIBULATION
DANIEL 12:1-13

In the Book of Genesis, the Lord brought Abraham outside and said: "Look now toward heaven and count the stars if you are able to number them; And He said to him, 'So shall your descendants be' " (Genesis 15:5). Daniel was told: "Those who are wise shall shine like the brightness of the firmament, and those who turn many to righteousness like the stars forever and ever" (Daniel 12:3).

What a message of hope! Those that are faithful to the Lord will shine like the stars. It had been revealed to Daniel all the distress and trouble that was coming. Many details of the last three and one-half years of the Great Tribulation are revealed in Revelation Chapters 6-9. There will be famine, disaster, and death. But the Lord God is in control of history, and He has a plan. It was revealed to Daniel that the Lord will provide a special messenger.

MICHAEL, A SPECIAL MESSENGER

"At that time" (Daniel 12:1) means the "time of the end" (Daniel 11:40). This will happen at the second coming of Christ. When the end approaches, "Michael shall stand up, the great prince who stands watch over the sons of your people" (Daniel 12:1). Michael, a great prince, who watches over Israel, the people of God, will stand up. Michael is declared an archangel in Jude who contended with the devil and said, "The Lord rebuke you!" (Jude 9).

Now if you were Daniel, and you had received word of all the problems and oppression that were coming, you might be discouraged and depressed. Then imagine how you would be relieved when you learned of God's messenger, Michael, coming to "stand watch over the sons of your people."

"A time of trouble, such as never was seen since there was a nation, even to that time" (Daniel 12:1b). This terrible period would be the Great Tribulation just before the coming of Christ. "And at that time your people shall be delivered …" (Daniel 12:1). Those that are delivered are those whose names are "found written in the book" of life. This is God's record of those who have been saved by faith. Jesus said: "Nevertheless do not rejoice in this, that the spirits are subject to you, but rather rejoice because your names are written in heaven" (Luke 10:20). John, in his vision of the great white throne judgment wrote: "And I saw the dead, small and great, standing before God, and books were opened. And another book was opened, which is the Book of Life" (Revelation 20:12). "And anyone not found written in the Book of Life was cast into the lake of fire" (Revelation 20:15).

Those who are saved are those who believe in the Lord Jesus Christ. The Book of Life is also mentioned in Revelation 13:8, 17:8, 20:12, and 21:27. Believer's names are written in the Lamb's Book of Life. The names that are included are those who have been forgiven because of the shed blood of Jesus Christ on the cross. They have placed their faith and trust in what the Lord has done through His death and resurrection. People were saved in the Old Testament time by faith in the Lord and what He was going to do. People are saved today by faith in the Lord and what He has already done for us on the cross.

SPECIAL FUTURE

1) Resurrection. "And many of those who sleep in the dust of the earth shall awake, some to everlasting life, some to shame and everlasting contempt" (Daniel 12:2). The word "sleep" is an expression for death. "In the dust of the earth" makes it clear he is talking about death. "And the Lord God formed man of the dust of the ground" (Genesis 2:7), and "For dust you are, and to dust you shall return" (Genesis 3:19). These two verses from Genesis describe God's creation of man from the dust of the earth and that when we die our bodies decay back to dust. There is no doubt that Michael was at this point talking to Daniel about death.

But then comes the startling statement: "shall awake" and "to everlasting life!" In the Old Testament times people believed that when a person died, they went to Sheol. Sheol was a dark shadowy place. Some began to believe that faithful people would be with Abraham, and Abraham was with God. The Book of Job is the account of the sufferings of Job. In the midst of his trials, Job came to believe a wonderful truth: "For I know that my Redeemer lives, and He shall stand at last on earth; and after my skin is destroyed, this I know that in my flesh I shall see God" (Job 19:25-26). This same wonderful truth was revealed to Daniel. Jesus said: "I Am the resurrection and the life. He who believes in Me, though he may die, he shall live" (John 11:25). When believers in the Lord Jesus Christ die, they go to be with the Lord (Revelation 14:3). Our resurrection involves our receiving a resurrected body like the one Jesus had after He arose from the tomb.

2) The judgment. The idea of resurrection brings with it the judgment. "Some to shame and everlasting contempt" (Daniel 12:2) implies the judgment. Jesus said the hour is coming when the dead will hear His voice and "those who have done good, to the resurrection of life, and those who have done evil, to the resurrection of condemnation"

(John 5:29). It was revealed to John that there is a second death in an eternal hell (Revelation 20:14).

SPECIAL REWARD

True believers live their faith, share their faith, and reflect the glory of God. "Those who are wise shall shine like the brightness of the firmament, and those who turn many to righteousness like the stars forever and ever" (Daniel 12:2). Paul wrote: "We are to shine as lights, holding forth the light" (Philippians 2:15). We can rejoice that we will shine like the stars forever. Daniel held out a hope to his people that was revealed to him by the Lord, that there was a future and a hope for His people. The Lord revealed a special messenger, Michael; a special future, resurrection to everlasting life for those whose names are in the Book of Life; and a special reward, that believers will shine like the stars forever.

That hope is our hope, because one day when the books are opened the big question is going to be: "Is my name written in the Lamb's Book of Life?"

SEAL IN THE BOOK

Daniel was told to "shut up the words, and seal the Book until the time of the end" (Daniel 12:4). The word "seal" means "to affix a seal." To make a document authentic, a king or official would apply clay or wax, stamped with an impression from a seal or a ring. The document could not be altered without breaking the seal. Daniel's prophecy was symbolically sealed (Daniel 12:9), meaning they were authentic and could not be altered. In Revelation the seal of the scroll of judgment is broken, because the time has come. "Who is worthy to open the scroll and to loose its seals?" (Revelation 5:2). "Behold, the lion of the tribe of Judah, the Root of David, has prevailed to open the scroll and to loose its seven seals" (Revelation 5:5).

Rapid Movement, Increase in Knowledge

Michael also told Daniel in relation to "the time of the end; many shall run to and fro, and knowledge shall increase" (Daniel 12:4). The increase in knowledge obviously applies to our day. It is almost impossible to keep up with all the advancements in technology and science. "Many shall run to and fro" is also true of our time. Americans seem to be constantly in motion. During the summer of 2021, we even had civilians traveling in space. I believe we are living in the last times and the next event on the "prophetic calendar" is the return of Christ for His believers. Here in Daniel, we have seen the description of the Antichrist and the evil times that will usher him in. This vision began in Chapter 10 when the angel Gabriel brought the vision of the end, with the Great Tribulation and the resurrection.

How Long?

As Daniel was standing beside the Tigris River, he saw three persons, one on each side of the river and one above the river (Daniel 12:5). The "two others" refer to angels apparently different from the angels Daniel had already seen. There was a "man clothed in linen, who was above the waters of the river" (Daniel 12:6). The description of the exalted Christ in Daniel 10:4-6 includes the phrase "clothed in linen" (Daniel 10:5). So the man above the river was an appearance of our Lord Jesus Christ to Daniel.

One of the angels asked the man clothed in linen: "How long shall the fulfillment of these wonders be?" (Daniel 12:6). "How long" may refer to the duration of the trials and not asking when the events would begin. The "wonders" may include end time events, such as the work of the Antichrist, the time of tribulation, the persecution of Israel and the final deliverance. I'm sure if we had been there, we would have asked the same question. The disciples asked Jesus that question: "Tell us when will these things be? And what will be the sign of Your coming, and the end of the age?" (Matthew 24:3).

"The man clothed in linen" lifted both hands up to heaven and "swore by Him who lives forever" that it would be "a time, times, and half a time" (Daniel 12:7). This period adds up to three and one-half years. This may refer to the time preceding the second coming of Christ (Daniel 7:25). This will occur when the "power of the holy people" has been "shattered" and "all these things finished" (Daniel 12:7). This seems clearly to mean the time of Christ's second coming and the final judgment.

Daniel did not understand this revelation to him and asked, "My Lord, what shall be the end of these things?" (Daniel 12:8). Daniel realized that the person speaking to him was the Lord.

THE CHALLENGE

Instead of an explanation, Daniel received a powerful challenge: "Go your way …" (Daniel 12:9). This is not a rebuke, but a challenge to keep on with the work that the Lord had called him to do. Daniel needed to keep on serving and obeying the Lord. "The words are closed up and sealed till the time of the end" (Daniel 12:9). The words were "sealed" as mentioned in Daniel 12:4. The words would be preserved like an official document. It did not mean to hide the words. The Lord had given to Daniel what needed to be preserved for the end times.

Daniel had work to do. Prophets did not just foretell the future, but they proclaimed the truth from the Lord about who the Lord is, and what He is in the world.

The Lord wants us to understand our times and proclaim to others that Jesus is coming. People need to repent and be ready. The Lord has never called you to study His Word just for yourself, but so you can be better equipped to share the gospel about the grace and forgiveness of the Lord, our need for repentance and faith. Jesus is coming again!

PURIFIED AND REFINED

"Many shall be purified, made white, and refined ..." (Daniel 12:10). This seems to be about the Tribulation time. A person has to be purified and refined. A person can't clean up their lives spiritually all by themselves. It is only by the power of the shed blood of Jesus Christ that anyone can be purified. A person can be "made white" or "made spotless." Sacrificial lambs had to be "spotless," without any blemish. A person is made "spotless" in the Lord's sight when he comes in faith to the Lord Jesus Christ. "Refined" refers to the process of purifying metal by intense heat and the dross. The impurities are removed. The dross, the bad in us, must be burned out, consumed so that we are pure, just like gold is refined in fire.

During the Tribulation, there will be those who respond in faith to the Lord Jesus Christ. Some will undergo these same trials and refuse to believe in Christ (Daniel 12:10b). "But the rest of mankind ... did not repent of the works of their hands ... and they did not repent ..." (Revelation 9:20-21).

NUMBERS

In Daniel 12:7, Daniel learned that the Great Tribulation would last three and one-half years. Different interpretations have been given for this number of days, "one thousand two hundred and ninety days" (Daniel 12:11). These days could possibly refer to the midpoint of the seven years of tribulation before the coming of Christ. Could the extra days be the time Jesus will set up the judgment?

Another number is presented in verse 12: "Blessed is he who waits, and comes to the one thousand three hundred and thirty-five days" (Daniel 12:12). No one knows for certain why the "blessed" is connected to this number or again what the meaning of the additional numbers may mean.

We must be careful about assigning significance to numbers when the Bible does not reveal the meaning. Some have tried to manipulate numbers to predict when Jesus is coming again. We should not do that. Remember Jesus said: "But of that day and hour no one knows, not even the angels of heaven, but My Father only" (Matthew 24:36).

There are still mysteries in the Bible. There are things Daniel and you and I don't know. We should look for Jesus' return, long for His coming, and be prepared to meet Jesus when He comes. But we don't know when He is coming!

THE PROMISE

1) Daniel was promised a "rest": "… for you shall rest" (Daniel 12:13). "Rest" was an Old Testament technical word that expressed God's promise to His people Israel. Rest was synonymous with the Promised Land. The Lord promised His people a "land flowing with milk and honey" (Exodus 3:8). But because of disobedience and idol worship they never really achieved all that the Lord wanted to give them. So in the Book of Hebrews it states: "There remains therefore a rest for the people of God. For he who has entered His rest has Himself also ceased from His works as God did from His" (Hebrews 4:9-10).

Jesus declared His promise: "In My Father's house are many mansions, if it were not so, I would have told you. I go to prepare a place for you" (John 14:2).

2) The second promise was "resurrection." "(A)nd will arise to your inheritance at the end of the days" (Daniel 12:13). The promise of resurrection is made to believers in the Lord Jesus Christ. Daniel was told he would receive his "inheritance." This inheritance was designated for Daniel. Paul declared: "In Him also we have obtained an inheritance …" (Ephesians 1:11). What a wonderful promise! This is the hope of all who believe.

My hope is that you know you have received this promise into your heart by faith and that you know you have an eternal home in heaven.

Have you learned anything from this study of Daniel that will help you live in these last days? After our journey through the Book of Daniel, you should be able to read the handwriting on the wall. We should be committed to putting our faith in the only One who can stand in this evil day and that is Jesus our Lord.

Will you stand with Jesus? The Lord still has work for His followers. It is exciting to awake to each new day and discover what the Lord has for us to do.

CPSIA information can be obtained
at www.ICGtesting.com
Printed in the USA
BVHW091543140622
639736BV00012B/966